FAMILY PORTRAIT

FAMILY PORTRAIT

A Play in Three Acts by

LENORE COFFEE

and

WILLIAM JOYCE COWEN

RANDOM HOUSE · NEW YORK

THIRD PRINTING

Shapiro
4.00
7-17-62 bpm
10-3-62 a

And he went out from thence, and came into his own country; and his disciples follow him.

And when the sabbath day was come, he began to teach in the synagogue: and many hearing him were astonished, saying . . . Is not this the carpenter, the son of Mary, the brother of James, and Joses, and of Juda, and Simon? and are not his sisters here with us? And they were offended at him.

But Jesus said unto them, A prophet is not without honour, but in his own country, and among his own kin, and in his own house.

St. Mark, 6: 1-4.

Family Portrait was produced by Cheryl Crawford, in association with Day Tuttle and Richard Skinner, on March 8, 1939, at the Morosco Theatre, with the following cast:

(In order of their appearance)

MARY, *mother of Jesus*	JUDITH ANDERSON
DANIEL, *son of Naomi and Simon*	RONALD REISS
JOSEPH, *son of Mary*	NORMAN STUART
A SHEPHERD	MAX LEAVITT
NAOMI, *Simon's wife*	VIRGINIA CAMPBELL
JUDAH, *son of Mary*	JAMES HARKER
MARY CLEOPHAS, *Mary's sister-in-law*	EVELYN VARDEN
REBA, *Joseph's wife*	LOIS AUSTIN
SIMON, *son of Mary*	TOM EWELL
JAMES, *son of Mary*	PHILIP COOLIDGE
MORDECAI, *a farmer of Nazareth*	WILLIAM FORAN
SELIMA, *mother of James and John*	KATHRYN GRILL
EBEN, *a peddler*	PHILIP TRUEX
MATHIAS, *a rich merchant*	HUGH RENNIE
A DISCIPLE	LEONARD ELLIOTT
HEPZIBAH	EULA GUY
APPIUS HADRIAN, *a Roman*	GUY SPAULL
ANNA	RUTH CHORPENNING
RABBI SAMUEL	BRAM NOSSEN
MENDEL, *a marriage broker*	WILL LEE
A WOMAN OF JERUSALEM	LOIS JAMESON
A CHILD	EUGENE SCHIEL
MARY OF MAGDALA	MARGARET WEBSTER
NATHAN, *a water-seller*	RONALD HAMMOND
DANIEL, *aged 16*	PHILIP TRUEX
ESTHER, *Joseph's daughter*	JOSEPHINE MCKIM
LEBAN OF DAMASCUS	GUY SPAULL
JOSHUA, *his son*	NEAL BERRY
BEULAH	RUTH CHORPENNING

Staged by MARGARET WEBSTER

Settings and costumes by HARRY HORNER

SCENES

ACT ONE

SCENE ONE. A house in Nazareth. Summer.

SCENE TWO. Wineshop at Capernaum. The following Spring.

ACT TWO

SCENE ONE. A house in Nazareth. A year later.

SCENE TWO. The same. The following week.

ACT THREE

SCENE ONE. A street in Jerusalem. Spring of the following year.

SCENE TWO. A house in Jerusalem. The same night.

SCENE THREE. The house in Nazareth. Some years later.

ACT ONE

ACT ONE

SCENE ONE

The courtyard of a simple carpenter's house in Nazareth. Upstage center is the main building, a low plaster house with a wooden door in the center. On the left corner of the house is a fig tree in full leaf, under which a round bench has been built. Farther to the left are a few stone steps which lead up to a wooden annex of the house. At the right side of the house is a wooden shed that is used as a carpenter shop. It has a carpenter's bench and tools. Above the shed is a wooden sign on which is painted the word CARPENTER. *At right is part of the plaster wall which surrounds the farm, the visible portion stretching from downstage right to upstage right. On the downstage right corner of the wall is a heavy wooden garden gate, which can be bolted with a heavy wooden bar. In the yard are a large table and numerous stools, benches, etc. In the distance are soft rolling hills and far away one can see the outlines of another little farm.*

Early morning. Just before the rise of curtain a cock crows. At rise of curtain the stage is empty. A little flutter of breeze rustles the thick leaves of the fig tree.

MARY *comes from the house with a tray of dishes and a tablecloth folded over her arm. She is a slight woman of about forty-five but looks younger. There are understanding and humor in her face, as well as sweetness and great character. She moves quickly and deftly. She puts the tray down on the*

3

seat under the fig tree and then lays the cloth, spreading it carefully. The cock crows again. This time it is answered by the bleating of sheep and goats. MARY *starts to put the dishes on the table. A small boy of six or thereabouts, dressed only in shorts, comes from the house, rubbing his eyes sleepily. He is dragging a small shirt in his other hand. He yawns as he says:*

DANIEL

Morning, Grandmother.

MARY

Morning, Daniel. How's my big helper? (*Sees him*) Gracious, child, aren't you dressed yet?

DANIEL

A button came off my pants. (*He backs around so we see braces dangle.*)

MARY

Your mother sewed it on only yesterday—

DANIEL

It came off again. I was out playing with the boys after school and—

MARY

(*Kisses him*)

—and you don't know how it happened? It just hopped off all by itself— (*Hugs him*) Never mind—we'll hold your braces with a pin—this once. But don't tell your mother! (*She takes a large pin from her belt and fastens brace to pants top.*)

JOSEPH'S VOICE

Hasn't that boy gone for the goat yet?

4

MARY

He can't until I fix his braces.

JOSEPH'S VOICE

Well, hurry it up, will you, Mother? We have to have
breakfast early this morning.

MARY

Yes—I know. (*Continues fastening*) There—I hope this
will hold—at least until you get home from school. What
did you learn there yesterday?

DANIEL
(*Putting on his shirt*)

Oh, lots of things. The days of the week—the months of
the year. You know, I think it's a waste of time for me to
learn all that stuff if I'm going to be a carpenter. I can
whittle like anything already—

MARY

There you are! Now hurry and get the goat, dear. (*She
stops, hears the shepherds' pipes*) The shepherds are out with
their flocks already. And we're in a rush for breakfast this
morning.

DANIEL

Do I have to go and get that old goat again? I got her yesterday. It's Esther's turn.

MARY

Esther had an earache last night. Aunt Reba's keeping her
in bed.

5

DANIEL

Well, I got her the morning before, too. And she *butted* me—*hard!*

MARY

You don't want her to butt Esther, do you? Especially with an earache.

DANIEL

That isn't where she butted *me!*

(MARY *goes over and kneels beside him and puts her arms around him. She speaks quickly, in a low voice.*)

MARY

Look, darling—it's very important that we don't upset anyone this morning any more than we can help.

DANIEL

Why?

MARY

Well—something happened last night that disturbed your uncles very much.

DANIEL

Father, too?

MARY

Yes. So I want everything to be as pleasant as possible— it will help me a lot. Now go along like a good boy—get the goat. (*She adds*) I'm baking cookies this afternoon.

DANIEL

I'll run!

(MARY *gives him a little hug. He exits and* MARY *starts to set the table with the breakfast things. While she*

6

is doing this, NAOMI *comes from the house. She is
an attractive young woman—amiable, rather imma-
ture. She is* DANIEL'S *mother.*)

NAOMI

I was thinking—the boys ought to have an egg for breakfast
if they're going to do that job out in the country. It's a
long way.

MARY

That's a good idea. (*Pause*) Simon up yet?

NAOMI

He's dressing.

MARY
(*Continues setting table*)
Did he—did he say anything when he came to bed last
night?

NAOMI

He kept me awake half the night talking. (*Adds impulsively*) You know, I think they ought to show *you* a little
more consideration—and I *told* him so!

MARY
(*Puts an affectionate hand on* NAOMI'S *arm*)
You're a good girl, Naomi—like my own daughter. But if
you don't agree with your husband—don't say anything.

NAOMI

Of course, Simon by himself wouldn't be so bad if Joseph
didn't keep him all stirred up.

7

MARY

Well, brothers are like that. Would you like to mix the porridge for me? That'll be a *real* help.

(NAOMI *exits and* MARY *picks up the small wood basket and starts toward the carpenter shop just as* JUDAH, *the youngest son, a boy of seventeen, comes down the stairs whistling. He is gay and charming and he and his mother are very close.*)

JUDAH

Morning, Mother. (*Comes over and kisses her and takes the basket*) Here—let me do that.

MARY

Morning, Judah. Early breakfast—

JUDAH

(*Talking over his shoulder*)

I know. Isn't it just like Mordecai? After holding back on that roofing job all Summer, he sends word last night that he wants the work started today. (*Starts putting chips in basket*) And he won't pay a cent more than the price we made when labor was cheap.

MARY

You'll have a hard time making money on it—but you may get other jobs through it.

(JUDAH *comes out of shop with a full basket of chips and starts toward the house, then stops.*)

JUDAH

What was the row last night? I heard old James going on at a great rate—so I slid off to bed—

8

MARY

(*Avoiding an answer*)

You were late coming home—

JUDAH

I went to see Miriam. And, Mother, what do you think?
Aaron let us talk together *alone*—for five whole minutes!

MARY

(*Smiling*)

And what did you say?

JUDAH

Oh, we didn't say anything. I just looked—and she smiled.
It was wonderful! (*Pause, then eagerly*) You know, I think
I'll take that job at Choraizon! If I'm going to get married, I'll
have to earn more money.

MARY

Married?

JUDAH

I'm going on seventeen!

MARY

So you are. Well, Miriam's a lovely girl. But are you sure
it's all right with her father?

JUDAH

Why not?

MARY

I always thought Aaron was kind of ambitious. Still, *we've*
nothing to be ashamed of.

9

JUDAH

Well, I told you he left us *alone!*

MARY

So you did. (*Puts her arm around him*) My baby getting married!
> (*The gate opens and a rather large, middle-aged woman enters. She is shrewd of eye, aggressive in manner— but kind. It is* MARY CLEOPHAS, MARY'S *sister-in-law and neighbor. She has a small bowl in her hand.* MARY *greets her with genuine eagerness and affection.*)

MARY

Mary Cleophas! My, but I'm glad to see you!

MARY CLEOPHAS

I just came to borrow some barley.

MARY
(*Hesitating*)
Take the wood inside, Judah. (JUDAH *exits to house.*)

MARY CLEOPHAS
(*Coming closer*)
Something's happened?

MARY

Yes.

MARY CLEOPHAS

What is it?

10

MARY

(*With a cautious look around*)

Jesus went away last night.

MARY CLEOPHAS

What did the boys say?

MARY

Oh, they're furious!

MARY CLEOPHAS

Well, I knew they would be. And I can't say as I blame them. (*Pause*) How'd it come about?

MARY

He just told them he was going. You know how he is once his mind is made up. Nothing they said could shake him. And he went.

MARY CLEOPHAS

I suppose they blame you.

MARY

Oh, yes. "I encouraged him"—"didn't think of my other children." I don't think breakfast is going to be very pleasant—no one speaking to anyone. Stay and have it with us. It won't be so bad with you here.

MARY CLEOPHAS

I never knew anyone to stop being unpleasant on my account—but I'll be glad to stay. (*Puts bowl down*) So he left! How long will he be gone?

MARY

I—I don't know—exactly—

MARY CLEOPHAS

You mean he didn't say?

MARY

(*Uneasily*)

I don't suppose he *knew*. He'll stay until he's done what he set out to do. (*Then, with a little rising panic in her voice at* MARY CLEOPHAS' *dubious expression*) He's always come back before! That time he went away with John—he came back, didn't he? And the forty days he spent in the desert—he came back. He's *always* come back—

MARY CLEOPHAS

Of course. I was just wondering. (*Pause*) I hope you did right letting him go.

MARY

If you could have seen his face! I never saw anyone look so happy. As if he was *ready* for something.

(*There is a commotion outside the gate.*)

DANIEL'S VOICE

Quick! Someone help me! (MARY *hurries to the gate, opens it and* DANIEL *tumbles in*) She got away! And she *butted* me—just like I told you she would! And in the same place, too! (*He rubs his little bottom.* JUDAH *comes from the house.*)

MARY

Go out and help Daniel with the goat, dear.

JUDAH
(Picks up jug and exits through gate)
Come along, young fellow. (DANIEL *and* JUDAH *exit.*)

DANIEL
I *hate* that old goat!
>   (REBA *comes out of the house. She is a little older than*
>   NAOMI, *handsome in a dark way, and inclined to take*
>   *everything very seriously.*)

MARY
Good morning, Reba—how's Esther's ear?

REBA
Better. I put warm oil in it. But the baby's having *such* a
time.

MARY
His teeth again?

REBA
(Nods)
What with his teeth and Esther's ear I've had an awful
night. And poor Joseph—*he* never slept a wink!

MARY
(Deliberately misunderstanding)
Well, when you have children they do keep you awake.
His father walked the floor many a night with *him*—

REBA
(Interrupting)
It wasn't that. Joseph was too *worried* to sleep. No one
realizes how high-strung he is—or they wouldn't upset him.

(*Turns to* MARY CLEOPHAS) You're out early, aren't you, Auntie?

MARY

Aunt Mary is having some breakfast with us this morning. Will you tell Naomi? (*To* MARY CLEOPHAS) We're having eggs—the boys have a job of work at Mordecai's. And it's a long walk. (REBA *exits.*)

MARY CLEOPHAS
(Busy at table)

I wouldn't let those boys bully me.

MARY
(Also busy at table)

I won't. But I *do* like to have things pleasant. It's hard on Reba and Naomi, too—they're such good girls.

MARY CLEOPHAS

Reba sounded a bit touchy.

MARY

Oh, well—you don't know what Joseph may have been saying to her. After all, they have to side with their husbands.

> (JOSEPH *enters. He is the third son in the family, usually breezy, energetic—a born "go-getter." This morning he is silently belligerent—only waiting for the word to set him off.*)

MARY
(With nervous cheerfulness)

Good morning, Joseph—breakfast's nearly ready.

> (JOSEPH *doesn't answer.*)

FAMILY PORTRAIT

MARY CLEOPHAS

Well, what makes *you* so gay and chipper?

JOSEPH

Oh, good morning, Aunt Mary. I didn't see you. (*He goes past her to the shop and disappears from view temporarily.*)

MARY

You see how it's going to be! (*Smiles*) I'll get the porridge. (NAOMI *comes out of the house with the eggs and puts them on the table. Now all becomes activity.* SIMON *appears. He is next to* JOSEPH *in age, eager to please— anxious to be on the right side. He, too, is far from cheerful. He passes* MARY *in the door and kisses her.*)

MARY

Morning, Simon. Sit right down. Everything'll be ready in a moment. (DANIEL *appears from the gate and makes a rush for the table*) Daniel, did you wash your hands after bringing that goat in? (*He shakes his head*) Run and do it quickly, dear.

DANIEL

They're clean—honest they are!

NAOMI

Do as Grandmother says.
(DANIEL *rushes into the house, stumbling as he goes.*)

MARY

I never saw a boy yet who wanted to wash. I think you were the worst, Simon. (*Smiles*) But they turn out all right. (*She exits into house.*)

15

SIMON

(*To* MARY CLEOPHAS)
What brings you out so early, Aunt Mary?

MARY CLEOPHAS

Well, I got out of the wrong side of the bed this morning, so I thought I'd come where I could have a pleasant breakfast.

> (SIMON *gives her a suspicious look, which she meets blandly.*)

SIMON

I hope you get it here.

> (JOSEPH *comes out from the shop*—REBA *comes from the house.*)

REBA

Esther's sound asleep—worn out, poor little soul.

> (MARY *comes out with a tray, carrying a bowl of cereal, spoons, etc. She puts it down on the edge of the table.*)

MARY

Breakfast, everyone! (*To the others*) Where's James? (*As she speaks* JAMES *comes down the steps*) Oh, there you are— breakfast's ready. (*Calls*) Judah! Got the milk?

JUDAH

(*Entering through gate with jug of milk*)
Coming! I've got to wash my hands. (*Exits to house.*)

> (MARY *turns from putting spoons around the table.* DANIEL *comes from the house, sits down.* SIMON *sits also.* JAMES *stands by silently. He is the eldest, next to* JESUS, *tall, austere and bigoted.*)

FAMILY PORTRAIT

MARY
(*Standing*)
Do sit down, everyone—before things get cold. Eggs, James?

JAMES
I'm fasting.
(MARY *is pouring milk into the cups set at each place along the table. The others start to sit down.*)

MARY
That's the second time this week.

MARY CLEOPHAS
For goodness' sake, James, unbend and have some eggs.

JAMES
(*To* MARY)
I'll take a glass of water. (*Sits down.*)

MARY CLEOPHAS
That sounds nice and hearty! (*Sits down next to* REBA.)
(*They are all seated now except* MARY. *There are* three *empty places.*)

SIMON
Pass the eggs, please.

JOSEPH
What's the matter with your reach? (*Passes them anyway.*)
(*There is silence, broken only by the sounds of spoons against plates and cups being put back on the table.*)

17

MARY
(*Eager to make conversation*)
I've—I've—some nice news for you. Something I think will
please you all—

JAMES
That will be a novelty.

MARY
I think Judah's going to get engaged— (*Pauses hopefully.*)

JOSEPH
So we lose another carpenter!

MARY
Oh, no—he'll live right here in town. It's Miriam—

JOSEPH
(*Brightening*)
Old Aaron's girl! Why, that's a good match!

MARY
(*Happily*)
I thought you'd be pleased.
(MARY *sits down.*)

NAOMI
(*Anxious to help along*)
She ought to bring a fine dowry. (*To* DANIEL) Daniel, not
so much in your mouth at once!
(JUDAH *comes out of the house in high spirits.*)

18

FAMILY PORTRAIT

SIMON
(*Greeting him*)
Well—well—well—so Judah's got a girl!

JUDAH
(*His face falling*)
Who told you! (*Looks around table*) Mother—*you* did!

MARY
(*Contritely*)
I didn't think you'd mind, dear.

JOSEPH
Our baby brother!

SIMON
Going to grow a beard, Judah?

JUDAH
(*Both pleased and confused*)
Miriam doesn't like beards.

REBA
(*Teasing him*)
How does she know?

JUDAH
Oh, Mother—make them *stop!* Besides, it isn't settled yet—

JOSEPH
It *isn't?*

MARY
Oh, it's practically settled. Aaron left them alone together last night—

19

JOSEPH
(*Pleased*)

We'll have to tell Mendel to get busy— (JUDAH *makes a gesture of annoyance*) You *have* to have a marriage broker to arrange about the dowry— (*Breaks off*) The rich shoemaker's daughter—our Judah's doing well for himself—

JUDAH
(*Hurt*)

I don't care *who* her father is—it's Miriam I'm thinking of— (*Sees empty place*) Where is Jesus, Mother? I wanted him to be the first to know. (*Passes plate*) Porridge, please—and lots of milk.

MARY
(*Nervously*)

Oh, I forgot—and set his place.

JUDAH

Isn't he having any breakfast?
(MARY *serves his cereal and pours milk on it.*)

MARY CLEOPHAS
(*To* MARY)

Doesn't the boy know?

JUDAH

Know what?
(JOSEPH *pushes his chair back and begins with gusto.*)

JOSEPH

It seems, my dear Judah, that your *favorite* brother has decided that he has other work to do—work much more impor-

20

tant than the mending of roofs and the building of barns—so he's left us with the Mordecai job on our hands without so much as a "by your leave"!

(MARY, *who is pouring more milk for* DANIEL, *puts the pitcher down on the table sharply.*)

MARY

That's not fair! You know he's been going to do this other work. You've always known—but you've kept him here time after time when he wanted to go. And as far as this Mordecai job is concerned, you know perfectly well that Jesus told you right from the beginning that he wouldn't be here to do it. You're all my sons, but it's time you learned to stand on your own feet and not rely on him for everything. (*She pauses, a little breathless*) Goodness knows he's the kind that'll carry as big a load as anyone'll give him!

JUDAH

You don't mean he's gone for good!

MARY

No, dear—of course not—

JUDAH

When's he coming back?

MARY

Well, that's hard to say, dear—

JOSEPH

He hasn't taken *us* into his confidence. We don't count. We're just his family!

21

DANIEL

What has Uncle Jesus done, Mama?

NAOMI

Nothing, dear.

DANIEL

Then *why* is everyone cross with him?

SIMON

Drink your milk—and don't ask questions. (*To* NAOMI) I wish someone would teach the boy manners. Personally, I've nothing against his preaching—but I don't see why he can't do it on Sundays—or when work is slack.

JAMES

If he wants to preach, why isn't he a rabbi?

MARY

He doesn't agree with all their ideas.

JOSEPH

Oh, he's going to startle the world with something new, I suppose! (*Adds sourly*) He's the best carpenter in the family. We won't get half the good jobs without him.

SIMON

And he knew how to get along with people. They liked to do business with him.

JAMES

Surely you must all see how unpleasant this is for *me*. After all, I stand for something in the community—

22

JUDAH

I'll miss him so! I'll be lost without him!

MARY

So will I!

JAMES

(*Disregarding this*)

His views and behavior are *so* irregular. It's embarrassing for *me*. After all, my friends are some of the most important men in town. As for these new ideas of his—we believe in the law, *according* to the law—and no deviation.

MARY

Then how's the world ever going to progress?

JAMES

It's better off without progress if you have to break the law to do it.

NAOMI

Come along, Daniel, you'll be late for school. (*He kisses* MARY; *exits with* NAOMI.)

JUDAH

I don't see why he hasn't got a right to his own life! He's thirty years old. And he's got a lot of good ideas, too! If people would live the way he wants them to the world would be a fine place! Room for everyone. And he's practical. Believes in paying people decent wages. Says a man is worth his hire. But not to worry about being rich. That there're other kinds of *riches* besides money!

23

FAMILY PORTRAIT

JOSEPH
(With sarcasm)

Hear! Hear!

SIMON

Quite the little orator!

MARY

Why shouldn't Judah defend his brother?

JAMES

What *I* want to know is—why did it have to happen to *us*?
Why did *we* have to have a fanatic like that in the family?

MARY

He's always had these ideas ever since he was a little boy.
You remember when he was only twelve and we left him in
the Temple—

JAMES

Yes, yes, Mother. We all know that by heart! And if he
hadn't been encouraged then he wouldn't be doing this now.
(Smugly) When *I* was a young boy—

MARY CLEOPHAS

Get out, James! You were *born* middle-aged.

MARY
(Haltingly)

You know—he always felt he had a special work to do. That
time he went with John—

SIMON

A fine end *John* came to!

24

MARY

(*Ignoring this*)

And when he stayed away those forty days—he'd made up his mind—

JOSEPH

We know, Mother. We had to listen to him—

MARY

Suppose he has gone out to spread his kind of thinking? After all, what is it? To be kind—to be fair—to love your enemies and do good to those that hate you. What *harm* can come of that?

JOSEPH

Not to *him,* perhaps—but what about us?

SIMON

Yes—we've built up a good business here—

MARY

With *his* help.

SIMON

(*Uncertainly*)

That's so, Joseph.

JOSEPH

So it gives him a right to ruin it?

MARY CLEOPHAS

Well, they say you never know a family till you've had breakfast with them. (*With decision*) You're making too much of the whole thing. He's gone away before—and he'll go away again.

25

JOSEPH

It isn't as if he had anything important to say! *Kindness!* You've got to startle people if you want to get anywhere—and who's going to be startled by kindness!

SIMON

(*Placatingly*)

I say—let him alone until he gets all this out of his system. Then he'll be glad enough to come back and pick up his saw—

JOSEPH
(*Quickly*)

He didn't take his tools with him, did he?

MARY

No.

JOSEPH

I've had my eye on that saw. (*Goes toward shop.*)

SIMON

(*Following him*)

I think I'll take his plane. Mine's pretty dull—

JOSEPH

Wait a minute! You got a new plane only last year. *I* ought to have this one.

SIMON

But you're taking the saw! You can't have them both!
(*During this action* MARY *and* MARY CLEOPHAS *start to clear the breakfast table.* REBA *exits.*)

26

FAMILY PORTRAIT

JOSEPH

We could cast lots for them.

SIMON

All right. But I'm certain to get the saw.

> (*As they are about to enter the shop there is a pound-
> ing at the gate.* MARY CLEOPHAS *admits* MORDECAI, *an
> excited, elderly man.*)

MORDECAI

You are all still here? Not started yet? Didn't you get my message last night?

JOSEPH

We're getting ready now—

MORDECAI

Getting ready! And half the morning gone! When it might rain any minute? And my grain all stored in the long barn— and you know how bad the roof is.

JOSEPH

Get the rest of the tools together, Judah. (*To* MORDECAI) Don't forget, Mordecai, that we've been after you all Summer about that barn while you shopped around to get the job done for less money.

SIMON

And when you *couldn't,* you came rushing back to us—and at a price made when materials were cheap.

MORDECAI

(*Changing his tone*)

Well, maybe I *was* wrong—but let's not waste time arguing now. It's been a bad enough year for the farmers as it is—

27

with the Romans telling us how much grain we shall plant—
and how many goats we can raise— (*He sighs.*)

MARY CLEOPHAS

But think of the pleasure you get out of kicking about it,
Mordecai. You know, I think one of the chief duties of the
government is to give the people plenty to kick about—then
they haven't time for their other troubles.

> (*During* MARY CLEOPHAS' *speech* JUDAH *has gone to the
> shop and returned with a tool hamper.* JOSEPH *and*
> SIMON *have got their tool-kits from the shop.*)

JOSEPH
(*To* JUDAH)

Did you put the plane in—and the saw? The ones that
belong to Jesus?

MORDECAI
(*Looks around*)

I don't see him. Where is he?
> (*There is sudden silence.*)

JOSEPH

Why—er—he's not here just now.

MORDECAI

The best carpenter in Judea. The reason I gave you boys the
job was on account of him.

MARY
(*To* JOSEPH)

Don't you think you'd better *tell* Mordecai?

28

MORDECAI

Tell me what?

JOSEPH

Well—er—speaking of Jesus—as a matter of fact—he's—er—he's gone away.

MORDECAI

Gone where?

JAMES

Our brother felt he had important work to do—

MORDECAI

Important! What's more important than my barn? It's the biggest barn in Nazareth! (*With dawning realization*) You mean he isn't going to be on the job?

JOSEPH

But we can get—

MORDECAI

You've swindled me! Cheated me! I'll have you up before the authorities— (*He pauses for breath*) It's off! The deal's off! (*Starts out.*)

JOSEPH

But you can't do that—we've got a contract!

MORDECAI

Sue me! (*Exits.*)

JOSEPH

(*Turning to* MARY)

There, Mother—*now* see what you've done!

29

MARY
(*Astonished*)

I?

SIMON

Telling him *now*—before we started the job—
   (MARY *stands for a moment, feeling the blame in the
   eyes of those around her, then steps to the gate with
   sudden decision.*)

MARY
(*Calling*)

Mordecai! Mordecai! Come back here!

MORDECAI
(*Offstage*)

What is it?
   (*There is a moment's silence while the brothers stare
   curiously at her, then* MORDECAI *returns.*)

MORDECAI

Well?

MARY

Just a moment, Mordecai! How did your agreement read?

MORDECAI
(*Triumphantly*)

That the work should be done by four sons of the House
of Joseph—

MARY

You'll still get four sons—Joseph, Simon, Judah—and James.

30

FAMILY PORTRAIT

JAMES
(*Startled*)

Why, Mother—surely you don't expect *me*—

MORDECAI

A lot of strength *he's* got after all his prayers and fasting! I won't have it!

MARY CLEOPHAS

Now, Mordecai. If a man goes to a dealer and orders four donkeys and doesn't specify four white ones—and three brown and one gray donkey are delivered, the law will hold him to the agreement.

JAMES
(*Stuffily*)

I don't call that a very happy comparison.

(*Before* MORDECAI *can answer there is a clap of thunder, followed by a few drops of rain.* MORDECAI *holds his hand out to feel the rain.*)

MORDECAI

Rain! Never mind *who* comes—my grain will be spoiled! Get my roof mended! Hurry, now! You, too, James! Don't get huffy!

(*All is excitement and confusion as* MORDECAI *and the brothers rush to get their tools and cloaks.* MARY *and* MARY CLEOPHAS *are left alone on the stage.* MARY *looks a little bewildered at the success of her strategy. She turns to* MARY CLEOPHAS *with a sudden pang.*)

MARY

Oh, dear—that wasn't wrong, was it? But when they all stood and looked at me—I felt we had to do something!

MARY CLEOPHAS
(*Drily*)

We did pretty well.
(*During this, all the brothers have collected their tools
and cloaks and gone out, but* JAMES *comes back.*)

JAMES

See here, Mother—I'll do this, even though I don't want to.
It's against my principles to work on a fast day—

MARY

Thank you, James.

JAMES

But—only on one condition—

MARY

What is it?

JAMES

If, within a reasonable length of time, Jesus doesn't give up
this notion of his and come back to his job here—we must
get him back. (*No answer from* MARY) You'll agree to that,
Mother?

MARY

Yes, James.

JAMES

And you won't oppose us?

MARY

No, James. (*She adds hesitantly*) And I—I appreciate your
helping us out.

32

FAMILY PORTRAIT

JAMES

And, Mother—

MARY

Yes, James?

JAMES

If the Rabbi asks for me, say I'm taking my brother's place—that I felt it my duty.

MARY

Yes, James.

(JAMES *exits and* MARY *sags a little.*)

MARY CLEOPHAS

Did he *mean* that about bringing Jesus back?

MARY

I suppose so.

MARY CLEOPHAS

And you agreed to it?

MARY

(*Hopefully*)

Maybe they'll forget about it. Maybe it will all just—blow over. (*Looks up at rain, shivers a little*) It's a cold rain. I begged Jesus to take his warm cloak. He'll be wet through.

(*At this point,* REBA *comes from the house and* MARY *quickly assumes an air of brisk cheerfulness and authority.*)

REBA

The baby's asleep. (*She wipes her forehead and upper lip*) My, I'll be glad when he's weaned. Nursing makes me perspire so!

33

MARY

I know. Sit down and I'll come in and warm something up for you.

MARY CLEOPHAS

I'll do it.

(NAOMI *enters, right, from taking* DANIEL *to school.* MARY CLEOPHAS *and* REBA *exit.*)

NAOMI

I've just talked to Daniel's teacher—he's doing *so* well in school.

MARY

Of course. He's way ahead of his age. (*Pause—then, forgetting* NAOMI) If he walked all night he must be at the Sea of Galilee by now. The place feels empty without him! (*To* NAOMI) It's going to rain the whole day. What do you say— we put up some fruit? We've all those peaches in the house—

(*She starts in the house with* NAOMI *as—*)

Curtain

ACT ONE

Scene Two

A wineshop in Capernaum. About noon.

The wineshop is built on a pier at one end of the Lake of Tiberius (the Sea of Galilee). The center part of the building is the wineshop proper with a bar, tables, stools, etc. At right is the entrance door leading in from the porch, which extends farther right. On it are a number of empty barrels. At the end of the porch some boats are tied. Inside, at upstage right, is a small bar, behind which are shelves full of jugs, bottles and other tavern equipment. Upstage center is a long table with a bench running its full length on the downstage side, so that the people sitting on it have their backs to the audience. In the back wall of the inn are two small windows. Downstage right and center are two tables with stools. In a wing of the room at left is another small table with two stools (for the use of MARY *and the disciple). At upstage left of the center portion of the inn is the entrance to the kitchen.*

At rise of curtain the seats are all full. EBEN, *the peddler, is displaying his wares to a woman.* AMOS, *a hungry-looking waiter, is waiting on the tables, while* SELIMA, *who runs the place, is busy in the bar.* SELIMA *calls to* EBEN.

SELIMA

Any signs of the boats yet, Eben?
        (EBEN *steps to the door and looks out.* SELIMA *yawns.*
        EBEN *turns back.*)

35

PEDDLER

There's a mist over the lake. I can't see past the shore-line.

SELIMA

(*With annoyance*)

The boys told me they'd be back in time for lunch. Heaven knows they made enough noise going out this morning! They'll have to be quieter if I'm going to spend all day and half the night on my feet running this business.

PEDDLER

Is your brother out of town again, Selima?

SELIMA

Gone off to Sidon—and with business so heavy here, too. Of course, this rush may not last forever. What would happen to this place here if Choraizon or Bethsaida made a good offer to Jesus? (*A customer pays for his wine; she hurriedly makes change, eager to continue*) The town of Capernaum does little enough for him—and he's the biggest attraction they ever had. Suppose some other town makes an offer and off he goes? What then?

PEDDLER

Does he show any signs of moving on?

SELIMA

No, but you never can tell. When he gets talking or walking you can't say when or where he'll stop. Take this morning. The boys should have been back from their fishing hours ago—but Jesus decided to go with them, and if he gets to making lessons out of things they'll forget all about coming

36

home. He may wind up on the other side of the lake and stay there! That's why I keep saying—"Sell now."

PEDDLER

Well—I don't know. Since things are going so well I'd stick it and take a chance.

SELIMA

Take a chance! That's a regular man's argument. Why take chances? I said that to my brother when he talked about making our house larger. "Why go to all the extra expense?" I said. "Jesus doesn't mind where he sleeps." (*She changes to a confidential tone*) I *must* say we never had anyone who was less trouble. Why, we once had John the Baptist and his followers at our house and they nearly drove us crazy!

> (*The servant passes with a cup of wine.* SELIMA *cranes her neck to look into the cup and then halts the servant with a jerk of her head. He comes close to her.*)

SELIMA

Haven't I told you a dozen times not to fill the cups so full? It makes a difference of a gallon or more on a busy day. I'll measure out the next lot myself!

> (SELIMA *exits to kitchen as* MARY, *accompanied by* JAMES, JOSEPH *and* SIMON, *comes to the wineshop door. It is obvious they have come a great distance, as they have on cloaks.* MARY *is a little timid and has lost some of her assurance of manner as we see her in these unfamiliar surroundings. She speaks quietly but firmly.*)

MARY

No, James, I'll wait here.

37

JAMES

But, *Mother*—

MARY

I've come this far with you, as I said I would. But I'm not going to embarrass my son in front of a crowd of strangers. (*Adds, a little choked*) I don't see how I could be expected to.

SIMON

After the scandalous things we've heard!

JOSEPH

There's no sense in not facing facts, Mother. He's simply out of his mind!

MARY

All the more reason for seeing him alone. I'm not going any farther.

SIMON

Maybe Mother's right—maybe we ought to wait and see him tonight—

JOSEPH

Then stay here with her! We're not going to wait. We came here to accomplish something and the sooner we do it the better.

JAMES

Don't you see, Mother—he's making himself and us ridiculous. It's time someone took him in hand. (*After a pause*) It's for his own good as well as ours—

MARY

Yes, James.

38

FAMILY PORTRAIT

JAMES
(After a pause)

Well—we're going.

> (SIMON *stands irresolutely for a moment, then as he sees they are really going without him, turns to* MARY.)

SIMON

You're sure you'll be all right here alone, Mother?

MARY
(With a little ironic smile)

Yes, Simon.

> (SIMON *hurries after his two brothers while* MARY *looks around for a place to sit. It is quite crowded and there is only one vacant seat at a table for two. Before she can take it a young man, with a serious, rather charming face, comes out from the kitchen entrance with a parchment in his hand and sits down and starts to write on it. He is obviously a familiar of the place.* MARY *stands a little to one side, trying to keep out of the way.* SELIMA *returns from the kitchen just as* MATHIAS, *a rich merchant, enters the wineshop. She rushes forward to greet him effusively, while* MARY *steps back out of her way.* SELIMA *brushes by without even noticing* MARY.)

SELIMA

Well, Mathias! Welcome to Capernaum! When did you leave Sidon? And how is your family?

> (As SELIMA *speaks she casts a quick glance around the room, seeking a place to seat him. There is no vacant*

39

seat, but one man has nearly finished. She taps him on the shoulder.)

SELIMA

You don't mind giving up your seat, do you? You've nearly finished and Mathias has come a long way. (*The man hesitates, but* SELIMA *has him by the elbow and half up before he can protest*) Here you are. (*She clears the table briskly*) What brought you here this time?

(*While* SELIMA *is busy seating* MATHIAS *the man who has been ousted from the seat grumbles to the man at the door as he stands eating from his plate. At the same time, another man who has been sitting beside the young man who is writing gets up, leaving a vacant place.* MARY *looks questioningly at the stranger who was ousted. With his mouth full he pantomimes, "You take it." She sits down beside the young man at the table next to that occupied by* MATHIAS. *The table is well downstage and* MARY *faces the audience.*)

MATHIAS

(*Sitting at table*)

A load of goods to sell—since they tell me everyone has so much money around here. And I've brought a fine appetite with me, too. How about a nice piece of fish? I've been traveling inland for the past month.

SELIMA

As soon as the boats come in, which should be any minute. How about a bowl of hot bean soup to warm your stomach while you're waiting?

40

FAMILY PORTRAIT

MATHIAS

Fine!

SELIMA

(*Calling to servant*)

Amos! A bowl of hot bean soup for Mathias.

(*As the servant starts for the kitchen* MARY *stops him.*)

MARY

(*To servant*)

I'd like a bowl of that soup, too—if I could—and some bread—

(*The servant nods and exits.* MARY *sits quietly listening to* SELIMA *and* MATHIAS, *shrinking back a little in her seat.*)

MATHIAS

How are the fish running, Selima?

SELIMA

Better than in years.

MATHIAS

Do you think this man Jesus has anything to do with it?

SELIMA

Do I think so? I should say he has! The old prophets used to pray and hope for God to do the rest. But do you know what this man does? He goes out and takes a hand at the nets. Like this morning. Whenever *he* pulls, the nets are always full. We only hope the price of fish keeps up.

(*There is a commotion at the front door. A man calls into the shop.*)

MAN

The boats are in!

SELIMA

(*To* MATHIAS)

Good—you'll be having your fish in less than no time.

(*A man in fisherman's garb comes through the crowd at the door, carrying a huge fish.*)

FISHERMAN

Here's a beauty, Selima.

SELIMA

Take it into the kitchen and tell the cook to give you a bowl of soup. Where are the boys? Are they coming in here to eat?

FISHERMAN

They're not hungry. (*Excitedly*) We had a fine catch! Enough for hundreds of people! (*He exits to the kitchen.*)

(MARY *listens to this and follows the man with her eyes as he exits.*)

SELIMA

(*Proudly*)

See? What did I tell you?

MATHIAS

(*Impressed*)

I'd like to meet this man myself. Where can I find him?

SELIMA

He'll be preaching—but you'd better get there early if you

42

want to hear anything. Otherwise, you'll get caught in a tangle of beds and stretchers—

MATHIAS

Beds and stretchers?

SELIMA

Cripples and invalids—they all go to him.

MATHIAS

And he cures them?

SELIMA

Certainly! And he's going to teach my boys how to do it, too. Then send them out by themselves. I don't see why they shouldn't be able to—once they've been shown how.

MATHIAS

But won't that take the crowds away from here, if people can stay home and see miracles performed right on their own doorsteps?

SELIMA

That's what I keep telling my brother. If they move on— where are *we*?

MATHIAS
(*A bit too eagerly*)

You don't happen to know where Jesus might be going next?

SELIMA
(*Suddenly cagy*)

I didn't say he was going anywhere.
(*The servant serves a bowl of soup to* MARY *and then brings soup to* MATHIAS.)

43

SELIMA

I'd better be seeing about your fish. (*She starts away, stops at the next table beside* MARY *and the young man and speaks patronizingly*) How's the soup?

MARY
(*Timidly*)

The soup is all right—

SELIMA
(*Aggressively*)

What's the matter with it?

MARY

It—it seems a bit thin—

SELIMA

You've got a country taste, if you don't mind my saying so. All city people prefer thin soup. (*Takes in her plain apparel*) I suppose you've come here to see our Jesus?

MARY

Yes—I have—

SELIMA
(*Partly for* MATHIAS' *benefit*)

Well, you've come to the right person if you want to get in touch with him. I can arrange it.

MARY
(*Impressed*)

You *can*?

44

FAMILY PORTRAIT

SELIMA

You see—my two sons are with Jesus, and we think the
world of him and he thinks the world of us. I suppose you
have some sons? (MARY *nods and starts to speak;* SELIMA *rattles on*) Then I'm sure you will agree with me it's very important for a man's future to have people like him. The *right*
people. Look at my father-in-law. When the Romans started
the new aqueduct at Sidon, he knew a man whose daughter
was the mistress of one of the officials—so he got a contract
for stone that made him a fortune!

MATHIAS
(Banging on table)
Look here! What about my fish!

SELIMA

By the time you finish your soup it'll be here. (*To* MARY)
You'll excuse me? (*She exits to kitchen.*)
  (*The young man, who has apparently been absorbed
  in his manuscript, looks up, meets* MARY'S *rather bewildered gaze, and smiles.*)

MARY
(A little wistful)
Does she really know so much about him?

YOUNG MAN
(A little humorously)
Well, naturally, her sons being with him, she knows a
little more than most people—but not as much as she pretends.

MARY

It's been wonderful to sit here and listen to all these things about him.

YOUNG MAN

If you're so interested, why don't you join the crowd and listen to *him?*

MARY

(*Confused*)

I'm waiting for someone. Besides, crowds frighten me a little—

YOUNG MAN

It's always like this. You'll never get a chance to see him alone.

MARY

(*Drawing him out*)

And they all believe in him. They all think he's wonderful?

YOUNG MAN

(*With glowing faith*)

For *me*—he's the beginning and the end.

MARY

Oh, I didn't mean *I* had any doubts about his being wonderful. I only meant—did the *people* think so—

YOUNG MAN

I can only speak for myself. I would *die* for him.

MARY

What does he *do*—that makes everyone follow him?

YOUNG MAN

Oh, nothing that I can explain. (*Searches for words*) He just sits out on a hillside—or in a field—and talks to people. And when they go away—they feel better.

(MATHIAS, *who has been listening intently between gulps of soup, gets up and comes to the table.*)

MATHIAS

Excuse me—but I couldn't help hearing what you were saying. Perhaps you can give me some information I want.

YOUNG MAN

Well—I don't know—

MATHIAS

Do you know anyone who has real influence with this man Jesus? One of the disciples?

YOUNG MAN
(*Simply*)

I'm one of the disciples.

(MARY *looks at him with added interest.*)

MATHIAS
(*Eagerly*)

Well, I've got a proposition I want to make to you. (*He looks toward the kitchen and then hurries on*) If you can get Jesus to leave this town and come to Sidon, I'll guarantee him all reasonable expenses—a salary for six months—and a nice bonus besides!

47

YOUNG MAN
(*Indignantly*)
No one would dare go to him with a proposition like that.
(SELIMA *enters from the kitchen with* MATHIAS' *fish and stands listening.*)

MATHIAS
Why not? It's perfectly sound. I'm a respectable business man—my word's as good as my bond.

YOUNG MAN
He wouldn't be interested.

MATHIAS
Nonsense. Everyone's interested in a good business deal. (*Lowering his voice*) If *you* could help me, I'd make it worth your while. How much? Come now—every man has his price—
(MATHIAS *suddenly becomes conscious that* SELIMA *is behind him. He straightens up, greatly confused, and fumbles for a pepper grinder, then returns to his table.*)

MATHIAS
Just borrowing the pepper—

SELIMA
How do you know it's going to need pepper when you haven't tasted it yet? No, Mathias—I was standing right behind you—I heard every word you said. (*Banging fish down on table*) And I know what you're up to! You've got your eye on Jesus and the business he brings. Well, let me tell you

48

one thing—neither you nor anyone else is going to get that
business away from here until we're good and ready to let
it go!

MATHIAS

It seems to me you're taking a lot on yourself—

SELIMA

Not any more than's been given me. You seem to forget
that my sons—

MATHIAS

Please, Selima—don't tell us about your sons again! And
as to business—Jesus isn't going to spend the rest of his life
here, is he? And when he does move on, he can move in *my*
direction, can't he? (*He adds slyly*) I might need a smart
woman to run the place—someone who knows how to handle
the crowds. (*He looks at the fish*) And feed them right.
(*There is a long pause*—MATHIAS *resumes pleasantly*) How
about my eating that fish while it's nice and hot? (*Sits down*)
There's no one can do a fish as well as you can, Selima.
(SELIMA *stands watching him*) Your brother's a lucky man.
I hope he gives you a good cut of the profits.

SELIMA
(*Complainingly*)

Not what he ought to—

MATHIAS
(*Mildly*)

You don't say? Well, that's what comes of doing business
with relatives. (*Takes a mouthful of fish*) My—my—what a
fish! And what a sauce!

49

SELIMA

(*Solicitously*)

I thought maybe it might need just a scrap more lemon—

MATHIAS

(*His mouth full*)

Not a thing—perfect!

YOUNG MAN

(*Seeing* MARY's *look of distress*)

Don't look so upset. These things happen all the time.

MARY

But what does Jesus think of it? Doesn't it make him angry?

YOUNG MAN

He knows how people are. How they have to struggle to make a living. He doesn't expect to change human nature overnight. Mind you—if anyone came to him *direct* with a proposition like that—(*he laughs*)—well, they wouldn't forget it in a hurry! But, even while he was angry, he'd understand—and make excuses for them.

MARY

(*Smiling*)

Yes—that sounds like him. Just like him. I remember once when one of his brothers tried to drive a sharp bargain—

YOUNG MAN

His brothers? Then you know the family—you must come from Nazareth. Do you know Jesus, too?

50

MARY

I know him very well. You see—he's my son.

YOUNG MAN

Your son! (*Looks at her intently*) Why, you know—there *is* a resemblance. (MARY *smiles*) And when you smile—it's quite like him!
(SELIMA *turns as she hears this and crosses over.*)

SELIMA

Quite like who?

YOUNG MAN
(*With innocent malice*)
Like our Jesus. There's such a resemblance between them—

SELIMA

I don't see it! And certainly no one knows him any better than I do—

YOUNG MAN

This lady is his mother.
(*There is a dead silence.* SELIMA *gulps, then struggles toward recovery. She flashes a guilty look in the direction of* MATHIAS *and then plunges in garrulously.*)

SELIMA

Oh, well—if you're his mother—you can understand why I was so upset just now. You've no idea how hard I work trying to protect him, just like he was my own son! (*She warms up to this idea*) The way people take advantage of him and try to use him! I don't know what he'd do if someone like me didn't step in and— (*Calls to servant*) A little

51

service here, Amos! Bring a portion of that fresh fish—tell the cook to have it piping hot. No, never mind—I'll go and fix it myself—then I know it'll be right. (*She bustles off to the kitchen.*)

YOUNG MAN

Did you see her face when I said, "This lady is his mother"?

MARY

I shouldn't have let you do it. (*Smiles a little*) But I *was* getting a little tired of hearing her go on as if he belonged to her! (*She pauses*) I can't tell you how glad I am I came here! (*Pause*) Wait until I tell my sons what people say about him! .

YOUNG MAN

Your sons came with you?

MARY

All but my youngest boy, Judah. He's away working in the country. He's going to get married. But he wouldn't have come with us even if he'd been home. *He* believes in Jesus—

YOUNG MAN
(*Startled*)

Don't the others?

MARY

Perhaps I shouldn't tell you this—still, you're one of his friends. (*In a lower voice*) You see, when Jesus left home, his brothers weren't in sympathy with him at all.

YOUNG MAN

You don't mean it!

52

MARY

Well, you know how families are. Then, to make things worse, we began to hear stories—from peddlers and salesmen traveling through—and finally the Rabbi himself came to see us. Well, from what the boys heard they thought he'd gone out of his mind. So nothing would do but they had to come here to take him in hand.

YOUNG MAN

You mean—have him give up his work? (MARY *nods*) But that's impossible!

MARY

Oh, I wasn't in favor of it. That's why I came along. I didn't know what they might do without me. But now I can tell them a few things— (*She turns toward the door*) There they are now! Oh, dear, I hope they haven't done anything foolish! (*She rises.*)

(*As* MARY *goes toward the front door* JAMES, JOSEPH *and* SIMON *enter. They look disgruntled, particularly* JAMES. JOSEPH *and* SIMON *give the crowded shop a quickly appraising look.*)

JAMES

Mother!

MARY
(*Enthusiastically*)

Wait until your hear what I've got to tell you. I wish you could have heard it all for yourselves—the most wonderful things! You'll be so *proud*—

53

JAMES
(*Furiously*)
Yes? Well, we've got something to tell *you*.

MARY
Why, what's the matter? Didn't you see him?

SIMON
We couldn't get close for the crowd.

JOSEPH
But we sent a message to him.

MARY
(*Apprehensively*)
What sort of message?

JAMES
We said simply, "Your mother and brothers are here and want to see you." And what sort of answer do you think he sent back—by one of those common fishermen?

MARY
I don't know.

JAMES
"*Who* is my mother—and *who* are my brothers?"

MARY
(*Incredulously*)
He said *what*?

JAMES
(*Enjoying repeating it*)
He said, "*Who* is my mother—and *who* are my brothers?"

54

MARY
(In a half whisper)
Oh, no!

JAMES
(His voice rising)
Ask Joseph here—

MARY
Sssh—not so loud!

JOSEPH
(Lower voice)
That's what he said, Mother. *(Pause)* A fine message to send to his own flesh and blood!

MARY
Did anyone hear him?

JAMES
Only about three thousand people!

MARY
Oh, there must be *some* explanation! He wouldn't do a thing like that for no reason!

JAMES
You always make excuses for him.

MARY
Is that *all* he said? Just—"Who is my mother—and who are my brothers?" *(Stumbles over words.)*

SIMON
Oh, no!

JAMES

As if that wasn't bad enough, he went on and made it worse.

MARY

Worse?

JAMES

There were people on all sides of him. You couldn't move edgeways—and what do you think he said, Mother? After he got our message he looked around at all of them and said, "*You* are my mother and *you* are my brothers!" To *them,* mind you! To that ignorant crowd!

MARY

(*A complete change of mood*)

But that changes everything! Why didn't you tell me that in the first place? Frightening me like this and making me think he didn't want to see me! With all those people listening he used our message to make a lesson of! That's the way he teaches. Don't you see?

JAMES

No, I don't see!

MARY

(*Her voice rising*)

But, James! That message wasn't for us—it was for the people who were listening. He was trying to tell them that because they followed him and his teachings *they* were his brothers and sisters—his mother, too!

SIMON

But, Mother—you don't understand—

56

FAMILY PORTRAIT

MARY

(*With increasing conviction*)

This thing about all men being brothers—why, he's said it to me hundreds of times! That's one of the things he believes in most! You'll see, when he's through talking to the crowd, he'll come here looking for us. And you ought to be glad you didn't get to him. What would you have said in front of all those people? "We want you to come home? We want you to come back and help us mend roofs and barns? We think you're out of your mind"?

SIMON

(*Timidly*)

I must say he seems to be doing well.

MARY

Doing well? Look at the crowds—that ought to tell you something!

JOSEPH

I'd like a chance to air my views and have a crowd follow me!

MARY

Why, an important man from Sidon was trying to get Jesus to come to his town—but the people here won't let him go. (*Her eye falls on the young man as she speaks*) And you should have heard what that young man over there thinks of him! He thinks the sun rises and sets in him. He said he'd *die* for him!

(*The* YOUNG MAN, *hearing himself referred to, turns and starts to rise.*)

FAMILY PORTRAIT

MARY

I'd like you to meet my sons— (*She pauses, then realizes she can't make the introduction and adds*) Oh, I'm sorry— I'm afraid I don't know your name—

YOUNG MAN

Judas. Judas Iscariot.

> (*The curtain begins to descend slowly as* MARY *introduces her sons, her hand confidingly on* JUDAS' *arm.*)

MARY

This is James—and Simon—and Joseph—

Curtain

ACT TWO

ACT TWO

Scene One

The house in Nazareth.
In bright sunlight, REBA *is taking freshly washed and dried sheets from the wall at background.* NAOMI *is seated under the fig tree, shelling a pan of peas. The girls are laughing at rise of curtain.*

REBA
(Folding a sheet)
I never saw her so excited before—

NAOMI
You'd be, too, if it was *your* son. I know how I'd feel if Daniel— But you're as excited as she is!

REBA
(Laughing)
Of course I am! And you are, too. Nothing like this ever happened to us before!

NAOMI
If only the boys get home—

MARY'S VOICE
(Offstage)
Naomi! Naomi, dear! Have you finished shelling those peas?

NAOMI

Almost. (*She turns to* REBA) Do you know, my fingers are all thumbs today—I'm *so* nervous!

MARY'S VOICE
(*Offstage*)
And, Reba! Are the sheets dry yet?

REBA

I'm just folding them.

MARY'S VOICE

Then put them in the lavender chest for a few minutes before you spread them on his bed. (MARY *comes to doorway and stands there for a minute*) Have Joseph and Simon come back yet?

NAOMI

Not yet.

MARY

They *would* be late on a day like this! Be sure and call me the moment they come. I want to tell them the news myself. I've got to watch that young lamb I'm roasting. (*She exits into house.*)

REBA

She wouldn't trust *me* with it. I don't suppose she'll let anyone else cook for him all the time he's here.

(MARY CLEOPHAS *hurries in through gate carrying four killed and plucked chickens in her hands.*)

MARY CLEOPHAS

Whenever there's anything important to do, all the men around here disappear! Joseph—Simon—where are they?

FAMILY PORTRAIT

NAOMI

They haven't come back from the country yet.

MARY CLEOPHAS

I thought they were coming home last night. And James? Where is he? Meditating, I suppose! (*Gesturing with chickens*) Can you imagine—I had to go all the way to the market to find someone to kill these birds. Where's Mary?

REBA

Inside—roasting a lamb.

MARY CLEOPHAS

Standing over a hot fire on a day like this! But I can't blame her. You should have heard all the things they're saying in the market place.

REBA

Are they excited?

MARY CLEOPHAS

Excited! That isn't the word! If you only knew the plans that are being made! It's the first time in all my years in Nazareth that I ever knew them to make such a fuss over the return of one of their own people!

REBA

It's a big honor for us, isn't it?

MARY CLEOPHAS

I should say it is! People spoke to me in the street who never looked at me before! And there were one or two I enjoyed snubbing! (REBA *finishes folding sheets and starts in the house with them.* MARY CLEOPHAS *hands her the chickens*) Here, take these in when you go, and get Mary away from that hot stove— (*Pauses as* MARY *comes out*) Oh, there you are!

> (MARY *is shaken out of her usual efficiency and stands uncertainly, speaking half to the others, half to herself.*)

MARY

I know I've forgotten something! Clean linen, water for the bedrooms, new wicks for the lamps—and I've my bread still to bake. Oh, yes—Reba, get out my best hand towels— with the blue embroidery—and put them in his room. And let me see—what else? Oh, dear—I must think!

NAOMI
(*Affectionately, to* MARY CLEOPHAS)
She's been going on like this for hours! (*To* MARY) Now, don't worry, Mother. Everything's going to be lovely. And, Auntie—you stay here and keep her from getting too excited. (*She exits.*)

MARY
(*To* MARY CLEOPHAS)
Coming home! I just can't believe it! Coming home!

MARY CLEOPHAS
If you don't sit down and rest a minute you won't be fit to see him when he gets here.

MARY
(*Sitting*)
I was never so happy in all my life! When I think how I

64

worried about him. The nights I've lain awake wondering if he was cold or hungry or—or *safe,* even. And now he's coming home! And not just coming, either. But *invited!* (*Pause*) Has—has anyone said anything about it in town?

MARY CLEOPHAS

Anyone? You're joking, Mary! Why, no one talks of anything else.

MARY

But we only knew it this morning—

MARY CLEOPHAS

They're certainly rushing to get ready for him! You should see the streets and the food shops! And the strangers that are here in town already! There won't be an empty bed in any of the inns by nightfall. People are coming in from the seacoast, too.

MARY

(*Happily*)

And all to see my son! I've been wishing all day I could be in two places at once. Home here fixing things for him—and out in the street hearing what people are saying about him. What *are* they saying?

MARY CLEOPHAS

I couldn't even begin to tell you! I don't suppose there's a mother in Nazareth that doesn't envy you, Mary.
(MARY *sighs—too happy to speak.*)

MARY

If only Judah were home—how he'd love to see his brother! Still, if things go here anything like they did at Capernaum, they'll never let him get away! (*Sighs again with sheer happiness*) You know, I'm trying so hard to be calm—to *look* calm, anyway—and then I suddenly remember the way he smiles and the way he speaks—and realize that I'll be actually seeing him—with my own eyes—*today!* And my heart just turns over! (*A little gasp.*)

MARY CLEOPHAS
(*Kindly*)
It's—it's been pretty hard for you, hasn't it?

MARY

Oh, I don't mean to complain. Other people need him. And, after all, I had thirty years. (*Pause*) I hope there won't be too many people around *all* the time. I'd—I'd like to have him to myself for a while. At first, anyway.

MARY CLEOPHAS

You haven't a chance. The house will be full of people who never knew we existed before!

HEPZIBAH
(*Outside the gate*)
Mary—Naomi—will someone open the gate—my hands are full.

MARY CLEOPHAS

There's one now! (*Opens gate*) Well, Hepzibah. What have you got there?

> (HEPZIBAH *enters courtyard with a stack of dishes. She is a large, voluble, middle-aged woman of dubious sincerity.*)

66

FAMILY PORTRAIT

HEPZIBAH

I just *had* to run in for a minute. I know how **busy you** are, with your boy coming home. Isn't it wonderful to have a son who's such a success? (*Puts plates in* MARY CLEOPHAS' *hands.*)

MARY CLEOPHAS

What am I supposed to do with these?

HEPZIBAH

(*Ignoring this and speaking to* MARY)

I thought you might need a few extra dishes—if you don't mind my being a little neighborly. There will be so many people coming—I've got some fine tablecloths, too—you're bound to run short.

MARY

Oh, thank you, Hepzibah. We *have* enough linen—but I'll be glad of the extra dishes.

HEPZIBAH

(*Rattling on*)

Have you got all the chickens you need? They tell me the market is sold out. But I don't suppose that should worry you. From what I hear, your son can feed as many people as come to him hungry. It must be wonderful having a boy like that.

MARY

(*Again trying not to be proud*)

I'm glad everyone says fine things about him.

HEPZIBAH

Fine things! You needn't be so modest, Mary. Not with

an old friend. If he was *my* son, I'd be shouting from the housetops!

MARY CLEOPHAS

I can believe that!

HEPZIBAH

(*Ignoring her*)

Do you suppose, after he's settled and you've had time to visit together, I could drop in one day? He *will* be staying here, won't he?

MARY

Where else would he stay?

HEPZIBAH

(*A little confused*)

I just thought some prominent people might want to entertain him. Still, this *is* his home. (*Pause*) Well, if there's anything else you want, just ask for it. It'll be a pleasure—

MARY

Thank you, Hepzibah.

HEPZIBAH

(*Exits*)

Well, good-bye.

MARY AND MARY CLEOPHAS

Good-bye.

MARY CLEOPHAS

I never could *abide* that woman!

68

FAMILY PORTRAIT

MARY

Still, it *was* nice of her to bring the dishes—
(JAMES *enters from upper floor of house.*)

REBA

(*From doorway*)

All the chickens are on the spits—

NAOMI

(*Offstage*)

Ask Mother if I should put butter in the peas now or later—

REBA

Naomi wants to know if she should—

MARY CLEOPHAS

(*Interrupting*)

Later.
(REBA *exits.*)

JAMES

(*Annoyed by the atmosphere*)

What's all the excitement? I spend a few hours in quiet meditation and come back to find everyone racing about and shouting—

MARY

Oh, James—*haven't* you heard?

MARY CLEOPHAS

Your brother's coming home today!

JAMES

Judah?

MARY CLEOPHAS

No, no! Not Judah! Your brother Jesus!

JAMES

What's he coming *here* for? Had enough of his tramps and fishermen?

MARY CLEOPHAS

I must say, James—you're never a disappointment! One can always count on *you* being disagreeable!

MARY

(*With quiet dignity*)

Jesus is coming back—by special invitation—to preach in the synagogue.

JAMES

Mother! Who's been filling your head with ideas like that?

MARY

(*Hurt—her voice a little unsteady*)

Go and ask Rabbi Samuel if it isn't so. He told Mary Cleophas himself, didn't he? It will be a big event— (*Her voice trails off.*)

MARY CLEOPHAS

The whole town knows it. Walk out and ask the first man in the street. Live in *this* world, James!

JAMES

(*Without conviction*)

I don't believe it! (*Pause*) But I'll find out.
(*Starts toward gate.*)

FAMILY PORTRAIT

MARY CLEOPHAS
That's taken the wind out of his sails!

MARY
I might have known that something like this would happen to spoil things.

> (MARY *rises and turns to* JAMES, *suddenly indignant.*
> SIMON *and* JOSEPH, *with their tools and bundles, enter
> as she speaks.*)

MARY
(*With spirit*)

And I'm not going to have it! This is his first visit home. He's been invited back here as an honored guest—and if the town can treat him that way, I think his own brother might do as much! (MARY *continues to* SIMON *and* JOSEPH) Come here, Simon! And you too, Joseph! You heard what I said just now to James? I mean that for you, as well! I want peace and quiet in this house while Jesus is here—and I mean to have it!

> (JAMES *stalks off, exiting through gate.*)

JOSEPH
But, Mother, *we're delighted!* We heard the good news as we came through town and hurried home to be the first to tell you.

SIMON
It's fine! He'll be honored by the whole community!

JOSEPH
He'll make this place famous! We're proud of our brother, aren't we, Simon?

71

SIMON

I should say we are!

MARY

(*Slowly*)

So—you're proud, are you? It's all right now, what he says and does?

SIMON

Of course, Mother!

JOSEPH

(*Heartily*)

Of course it's all right! Why, everybody believes in him— they're making tremendous plans for Sunday. (*Suddenly, to* SIMON) Say, they might call on us for a word or two!

SIMON

(*Both pleased and alarmed*)

What'll we say if they do?

JOSEPH

(*Walking toward shop*)

Oh, just something about how honored we are—our brother's worth at last being recognized by his home town —and that Nazareth's chief claim to fame may be that he was born here. (SIMON *laughs*) And then use that to lead into something about ourselves—and our business here—

(SIMON *and* JOSEPH *exit to carpenter shop with their tools, very pleased with themselves at the prospect of their coming prominence.*)

MARY

(*Half to herself*)

So it's all right now—since everyone believes in him—

72

FAMILY PORTRAIT

MARY CLEOPHAS

Well, that's one thing off your mind. You know how
they'll behave. I think I'd have more respect for them if
they'd stuck to their honest opinions, like James.

REBA
(*Offstage*)

Mother! Oh, Mother! Will you come here?

MARY

What did I tell you? I said you couldn't trust those girls
to cook a lamb if there's any excitement! A chicken, yes—
but a lamb! I'll have to do it myself.

(*As she starts to exit,* MARY CLEOPHAS *stops her and
puts her arm around her.*)

MARY CLEOPHAS

Happy, aren't you?

MARY

I feel that I'm asleep—that I'm dreaming—and I'll suddenly awake and find he isn't coming. Oh, dear! I *am* happy!
And I mustn't cry—or my eyes will be a sight—

REBA'S VOICE

Mother!

MARY

Coming, Reba!

MARY CLEOPHAS

(*Hurries into home as* JOSEPH *enters from carpenter shop*)
Well, Joseph, you just got back from that job in time.

73

JOSEPH

A piece of sheer luck. Simon wanted to come home by way of Choraizon and see Judah and get some firsthand news of him for Mother. But I'd lined up a big job here— (*adds importantly*)—with the Romans—

MARY CLEOPHAS

Doing business with the *Romans?* James will never agree to it!

SIMON
(*Coming from shop*)
That's just what *I* said! After all, it is a big departure!

JOSEPH
(*Angrily*)
If James wants to run the shop, let him come and work in it! *You* can do as you like—but when Appius Hadrian comes I'm going through with the deal!

SIMON
(*Anxiously*)
I'm not opposing you, Joseph. I'm just trying to tell you not to count too much on it until you see what James says.

JOSEPH

Do something for us, Aunt Mary—try to keep James out of the way while the Roman's here—

MARY CLEOPHAS

He's not coming *today*, is he!

JOSEPH

I can't help it! I made the appointment before I knew anything about Jesus coming home— (*Knock*) If that's *him*, Simon—*agree* with what I say— (*Goes to gate.*)

MARY CLEOPHAS

That's easy. Simon spends his life agreeing with everybody.

(JOSEPH *opens the gate and a rather resplendent Roman steps in. He raises his right hand in the old Roman salute.*)

APPIUS HADRIAN

Hail, Caesar!

JOSEPH
(*Clumsily repeating gesture*)

Hail, Roman! (*He nudges* SIMON *who makes a feeble gesture and mumbles something.*)

(MARY CLEOPHAS *chooses this moment to blow her nose with a trumpet-like sound. The Roman starts and looks.* MARY CLEOPHAS *returns his look coolly.*)

APPIUS HADRIAN
(*Pulls fig on fig tree*)

Well, come to any decision?

JOSEPH

I've been talking it over with my brother here. He's *very* enthusiastic—aren't you, Simon?

SIMON
(*Amiably*)

Yes—yes, indeed.

(*During the above* REBA *comes out of the house with a basket of linen and goes up outside staircase to*

75

*upper room. The Roman pauses in spitting out a fig
stem to stare at her legs.*)

APPIUS HADRIAN

When you get up here in the hill country you see better
legs on the women. (*His hand curves*) Who's the girl?

JOSEPH
(*Half flattered, half annoyed*)

My wife.

MARY CLEOPHAS
(*In hoarse whisper to* SIMON)

That's Roman culture for you! Legs! (*Exits house.*)

APPIUS HADRIAN
(*Pulling another fig*)

The best figs I've had in Nazareth.

SIMON

My father planted that tree.

JOSEPH

We'd be very glad to let you have a basket of them—

APPIUS HADRIAN
(*Spitting out a stem*)

Send them to my house.
(*Throughout this scene he eats figs and spits out
stems.*)

JOSEPH

Now, about the crosses. There're one or two little points
to be cleared up. First, how many would you need?

FAMILY PORTRAIT

APPIUS HADRIAN

Oh, about three a week. That's— (*Spits out another stem.*)

JOSEPH
(*Adding quickly*)
A hundred and fifty-six a year.

APPIUS HADRIAN

Better say a hundred and fifty. Call it three a week for fifty weeks. (JOSEPH *and* SIMON *exchange pleased glances, then* SIMON *looks fearfully behind him to see if anyone is coming out of the house*) But understand—sound timber, and according to specifications. We had trouble with one contractor last year. A number of his crosses broke in the joins and spoiled the show.

JOSEPH

You won't find that trouble with us. My father was an expert on joins. He always said, "If the join is good, the job is good." (*He pauses*) And the price?

APPIUS HADRIAN

I'm figuring in the fees and taxes with the price—

SIMON

More fees? We pay so many—

APPIUS HADRIAN

You'll pay more before long. It takes money to administer the country. To give you a strong government, police, army, navy, costs a pretty penny. What's fairer than you should pay for what you get?

SIMON
(*Intimidated*)
Of course. That's right.

JOSEPH
Simon—please don't interrupt!

APPIUS HADRIAN
(*Sits on edge of table and figures on tablet*)
Ten percent for my office—ten percent for the Public Works
office in Jerusalem—eight percent for the—
>   (NAOMI *comes from house and calls up toward roof-top.*)

NAOMI
Reba! *Reba!* Don't stay up there all day! Mother needs you
in the kitchen!
>   (JOSEPH *signals her to be quiet.*)

REBA
(*Answering*)
Coming right down!
>   (NAOMI *exits back into house and* REBA *starts running downstairs.* APPIUS HADRIAN *looks at her legs again.*)

JOSEPH
We're a little excited today. Our brother's coming home—

SIMON
And he's the best carpenter in all Judea!

APPIUS HADRIAN
Let me see—where was I? Oh, yes—eight percent for the

78

Department of Administration—four percent to the Department of Justice—and twelve percent to the Department of Public Amusements—then the inspectors—and local tithes—makes fifty-four percent—

(JAMES *comes from gate, unnoticed.*)

JOSEPH

I tell you, *I'm* going ahead and if James doesn't like it—it's just too bad— (SIMON *sees* JAMES *enter and nudges* JOSEPH, *who turns, suddenly aware that* JAMES *is listening to him.* JOSEPH *crosses to* JAMES) Oh, James, we were just speaking of you. This gentleman is Appius Hadrian. He's making us a very interesting proposition— (JAMES *ignores* JOSEPH, *and strides toward the Roman,* JOSEPH *talking as they go*) —one that we can't afford to let slip. Can we, Simon?

SIMON

No, indeed, James. It's—

JAMES
(*To* APPIUS HADRIAN)
We don't do business with foreigners.

APPIUS HADRIAN

This is a *Roman* province. And wherever the *Romans* are the other people are the foreigners.

JAMES
(*Ignoring this*)
In my elder brother's absence I am the head of the house and I forbid any dealings with the Romans.

79

JOSEPH

Now, look here, James! I'm not going to have you interfering! It's none of your business how we run the shop!

SIMON

You *are* being unreasonable, James—

JAMES

I will not have this place contaminated.
(APPIUS HADRIAN *rises and prepares to leave.*)

JOSEPH
(*To* JAMES)

You're taking too much on yourself! (*To* APPIUS HADRIAN) I hope you won't call the deal off because of my brother's bigotry! He's not a carpenter, you know—

APPIUS HADRIAN

Settle that between yourselves and when you're through wrangling let me know. (*To* JAMES) If Romans did menial work, such as carpentry, we wouldn't have come to you. (*Eats another fig—turns to* JOSEPH) Your figs are really excellent. (*He exits majestically.*)
(JOSEPH *turns to* JAMES, *his voice shaking with anger.*)

JOSEPH

You've gone too far this time, James! It's all very well for you to be righteous and pull a long face at doing business with the Romans. But Simon and I have families to support. Our wives and children—and you, too, if it comes to that! Simon, call Mother! We'll settle this thing once and for all!

FAMILY PORTRAIT

SIMON
(Going toward house)
Mother! *Mother!*

JAMES
She'll agree with me.

JOSEPH
We'll see about that.

MARY'S VOICE
What is it?

SIMON
Will you come out here?

MARY'S VOICE
I can't, Simon—I'm busy with my bread. Can't it wait?

JOSEPH
No. It's something that's got to be settled right now.

MARY'S VOICE
(Half-humorously)
Oh, dear. All right.

JOSEPH
(To JAMES)
We've carried the load in this house long enough. And we don't mind—if we're let alone. Do we, Simon?

SIMON
(Hesitantly)
I don't think you realize, James, how keen competition is getting.

FAMILY PORTRAIT

(MARY *enters, her hands covered with dough. She surveys them, laughing.*)

MARY

Just let me get my hands in flour, and that's the signal for everyone in the house to want something! All right—what is it that can't wait? (*She looks from one to the other*) Well, who's going to speak first?

JOSEPH

You see, Mother—the whole thing is so unjust. You know how long I've been trying to get some really big contract that would carry us over the slow times? I don't want to be a one-horse carpenter all my life!

MARY
(*Smiling*)

Yes—I know, Joseph. So?

JOSEPH
(*Warming up*)

Well—I pull strings and work everyone I know to get in touch with the Roman—

MARY

What Roman?

JAMES

I don't wonder you're surprised! He wants us to have dealings with—

MARY

I'll listen to you when your turn comes, James. Joseph is having his say now. Go on, Joseph.

82

JAMES

I've *had* my say! (*Stalks off upstairs.*)

MARY

Poor old James! (*Smiles*) He means well. What's the trouble now?

SIMON

He wants to run this shop from a seat in the synagogue!

JOSEPH

I say, if he wants to run it—let him come and work in it.

MARY

(*With gentle humor*)

I think you're better off leaving him in the synagogue. (*She pauses a minute to scrape some dough from her fingers*) There's something about the Pharisee point of view that prevents James from hitting a nail on the head. (*Seeing* NAOMI *coming out of house*) Oh, just a minute, Naomi, dear. Get my dough and mixing board, will you? I may as well do it out here. (*Turns back to* JOSEPH) All right, Joseph.

JOSEPH

I finally saw him and got him to make us a really wonderful proposition. I talked it over with Simon—who wasn't sure. You know how Simon likes to be on the safe side—

MARY

That'll do, Joseph.

JOSEPH

Well, anyway—I even got Appius Hadrian to come here himself! And I assure you he doesn't go everywhere—

83

MARY

Appuis Hadrian? Oh—he's the Roman—

JOSEPH

Now, don't say you haven't heard of him! I never saw such a family! He's the Public Administrator for the District of Nazareth!

MARY

Well, maybe I *have* heard of him—now that you mention it. (NAOMI *brings the bowl and board.* MARY *takes them and puts them on the table*) Thank you, dear. (*Starts kneading the dough*) Yes—Joseph?

JOSEPH

It's not much use my talking to you if you're going to have your mind on that bread!

MARY

(*Serenely*)

If I couldn't do more than one thing at a time, how do you suppose I managed to bring up a large family? Go on—I'm listening.

JOSEPH

Well, I go to all this trouble—have the deal ready to close—and what thanks do I get? Appius Hadrian insulted by that strait-laced old fogey! (*He mimics* JAMES) "We don't do business with foreigners!" And a nice fat contract slips right out of our hands!

MARY

A contract for what?

84

FAMILY PORTRAIT

For crosses.

MARY

Crosses?

JOSEPH

Now, Mother—you know perfectly well what crosses are!

MARY

Joseph! I'm not deaf!

JOSEPH

I'm sorry. But James has me all upset. (*A slight pause*)
You know—the crosses the Romans use for executions.

SIMON

They hang criminals on them—and nail their hands and
feet. (*He extends his arms*) Like this!

MARY
(*With a little shiver*)

Don't, Simon!

SIMON

Well, I'm just telling you.

JOSEPH

Besides—that isn't what James objects to—it isn't the crosses
—it's the Romans!

MARY
(*Puzzled*)

But I can't understand why the making of a few crosses is
such a big contract—

JOSEPH

A few? You don't call a hundred and fifty a year a few!

MARY

So *many!*

SIMON

They ship them all over the country. And they don't use the same ones over again. They leave them standing until—

MARY

Simon! Please!

JOSEPH

There wouldn't be any profit in it if the crosses were used more than once. (*Eagerly*) So you see what a good thing it is!

MARY

No, I don't! I'm surprised at you, Joseph, wanting anything to do with it. (*He starts to speak but she halts him with a gesture*) I'm not blaming you for trying to get ahead—it's your nature to be like that. But I don't believe in killing people—no matter what they've done.

JOSEPH

Only the lowest sort of criminals—

MARY

Even so. What have we to do with a business like that? And today—of all days! Jesus coming home—the whole town making ready to welcome him—and you sit here talking about Roman crosses! (JOSEPH *tries to speak but she cuts him short*) Now, I'm not going to discuss it any further. I've got too much to do! (*Calls*) Naomi! (*Pats dough into its final shape resolutely.*)

SIMON
(*To* JOSEPH, *trying to placate him*)
But, Joseph—maybe we won't need the contract with Jesus coming home. With the crowds that'll be here, everyone will want new things—

JOSEPH
(*Brightening*)
Maybe you're right.
(NAOMI *enters from house.*)

MARY
(*To* NAOMI)
Here, dear, take this in and put it in the oven.
(*Before* NAOMI *can go into the house,* DANIEL *appears on the top of the wall and stands flapping his arms like wings and crowing like a rooster.*)

DANIEL
Am I proud! (*Crows again*) And don't all the boys envy me! (*Jumps down, half tumbling, and lands with a clatter.*)

NAOMI
How often have I told you not to jump that wall? You'll fall and hurt yourself one day.

MARY
(*Hugging the boy*)
All the boys have jumped that wall—and none of them was ever hurt. So don't worry about Daniel.

DANIEL

You know, lots of the boys have had their fathers or uncles read in the synagogue. That's nothing! But not one of them was ever invited to preach—were they? Not even Uncle James—was he? (*Takes deep breath*) Won't I be important? And if you knew the boys who want to come and play with me after school so they can drop in when Uncle Jesus is here— (*Pauses breathless*) Got anything to eat?

NAOMI

Where are the onions I sent you for?

DANIEL
(*Blankly*)

Onions?

NAOMI

Didn't you get them?

DANIEL

I forgot.

NAOMI

Daniel!

SIMON

The boy just hasn't any head—goes around in a daze!

MARY

How can the child be expected to remember anything on a day like this? (*To* DANIEL) Go and get them now, dear. And if you go by the back door, you might find some cookies—

DANIEL

Thanks, Grandmother. (*Exits through gate.*)

88

FAMILY PORTRAIT

NAOMI
(*Half smiling*)
It's a disgrace—the way you spoil him.

MARY

Nothing of the sort. Boys need encouragement. They're much shyer than girls. (JOSEPH *and* SIMON *laugh;* MARY *turns toward them*) You needn't laugh. That's quite true. (*To* NAOMI) I never had to worry about my girls. They both found good husbands for themselves. Of course, I wish they lived a little closer, but I suppose a man must stay where his business is. But my boys . . . I'll never forget how the whole family sat up nights with you, Simon, while you were trying to get up courage to propose to Naomi. No, boys need to be helped along. (*A woman's voice is heard outside and* MARY *starts hurriedly toward house*) Oh, dear—if people keep coming I'll *never* get anything done! Let me get in the house before—

> (*The gate is flung open and* ANNA, *another neighbor, a smaller, younger woman than* HEPZIBAH, *appears with* EBEN, *the peddler, in tow.*)

ANNA
Oh, Mary! Come on, young man. Don't let your feet stick to the ground! I want my friend to see these things before they go out of fashion!

MARY
Well, Anna—this *is* a surprise!

PEDDLER
Here are all the latest styles—why go to Jerusalem when I

bring Jerusalem to you? (*Laughs at his own wit, dumps his pack and starts to display his wares.*)

ANNA

(*Effusively to* MARY)

He's got the loveliest things! You ought to see the new dress *I* bought! I don't know what my husband will say—my spending so much—but an occasion like this doesn't happen every day. What are *you* going to wear?

MARY

When?

ANNA

When? Why, Sunday when he preaches! Everyone'll be there!

MARY

Why, I don't know. I hadn't thought. I haven't anything new—

ANNA

(*To* PEDDLER)

See—I brought you to the right place! (*To* MARY) I've got to run along but make him show you his whole line of goods—

(MARY CLEOPHAS *comes from house as* ANNA *starts toward gate.*)

ANNA

(*Going off right*)

Good-bye!

90

FAMILY PORTRAIT

MARY
(*A little embarrassed*)
Thank you, Anna. Good-bye. (*To* PEDDLER) I'll be glad to look—though I haven't much time—

PEDDLER
(*Spreading wares out*)
This is your chance to get the smartest things at half the cost in your local shops. Everything new, everything fresh.

MARY CLEOPHAS
(*Coming forward*)
You've got a pretty expensive line of goods there, young man.

PEDDLER
(*Pulling out a scarf*)
Now, look at this scarf. Sunset, *I* call it. Have you heard the pagan verse about sunset?

"Sunset—it dips into the somber inkpot of the night,
  O! gracious sun which will appear again tomorrow
  In brighter colors."

MARY
(*To* MARY CLEOPHAS)
Do you think it would be very extravagant if I bought a new shawl—just to throw around the shoulders?

PEDDLER
Just a minute, lady. (*Dives into stock and holds up striped scarf.*)

MARY

Not too expensive—

MARY CLEOPHAS

Oh, that's pretty!

PEDDLER

Pretty! It was a sensation at the circus last Fall. The lady who wore it rode on a zebra.

MARY

It's a little conspicuous— (*Meanwhile, the* PEDDLER *brings out a blue scarf*) Oh, that's the prettiest of all! Blue! His favorite color! How much is that one?

PEDDLER

Ten pieces of silver.

MARY

It's lovely—but I can't afford it.

PEDDLER

If I was the mother of your son, there's nothing I couldn't afford.

MARY

You know my son?

PEDDLER

Know him? I'd be starving to death if it wasn't for him.

MARY

He helped you? Tell me about him.

92

PEDDLER

When I say he helped me—I mean—well, wherever he goes there's crowds—and where there's crowds there's money. Sometimes I get so interested in what he says I almost forget to sell my goods! He certainly knows how to hold people— right in the palm of his hand. (*Adds sheepishly*) You know, I listen to him and I think to myself—I won't drive such a sharp bargain next time—think of the other fellow, like he says. Then I get away and get mixed up in a business deal— and, well, I guess I forget all about it. You know how it is. (*Then, with a burst of generosity*) Look, since you're his mother—I'll make you special prices. The blue scarf—nine pieces of silver. Sunset—seven pieces—

MARY

I'll take it. The blue one. (*To* MARY CLEOPHAS) Oh, dear— maybe I shouldn't! But I *do* want to look my best. (*She reaches in pocket of her dress and counts out the money; then picks up the shawl and throws it around her shoulders*) Do you think he'll like it?

> (*She turns around for* MARY CLEOPHAS *to get its full effect, her back to the gate. Suddenly* DANIEL *bursts in.*)

DANIEL

He's here! He's here!
> (MARY *turns around so swiftly that the shawl slips unheeded from her shoulders.*)

MARY

Where? Where is he?

FAMILY PORTRAIT

DANIEL

Coming up the road! He's here! Mother! Father! Uncle
Joseph! He's here! (*He disappears into the house.*)

> (MARY *goes to the open gate—stands for one moment,
> looking. Then her arms fly out as she almost runs
> out into the road. The* CURTAIN *starts down. The*
> PEDDLER *kneels, doing up his pack, and* MARY CLEOPHAS
> *picks up the forgotten shawl and starts out after her.*)

Curtain

ACT TWO

Scene Two

A house in Nazareth.

At rise of curtain the stage is absolutely empty. There is no sign of life either in the courtyard or from the house. After a moment there is a knocking at the gate, but no one answers. The knocking is repeated and after another moment's silence the gate opens cautiously, disclosing HEPZIBAH. *She steps into the courtyard and takes a quick appraising look around.*

HEPZIBAH

Empty as a grave! (*Sees* ANNA *over wall*) Hello, Anna! Come on *in*.

ANNA

(ANNA *enters, hesitating yet eager*)
Do you think we should?

HEPZIBAH

They ought to be glad anyone comes to see them—after last Sunday. *That* was a frost!

ANNA

It certainly fell flat. It was good for the cake and sweet sellers, though. The crowd bought a lot. (*Looks around curiously.*)

95

HEPZIBAH

Even more than if he'd really performed the miracles. They got so tired of waiting for things to happen they ate everything in sight. (*Goes toward shop*) Well, if you ask me, I was glad to see this family put in its place. The airs they put on when they heard he was coming.

ANNA

Not James.

HEPZIBAH

No, I'll say that for James. He was never taken in by Jesus. (*In doorway of shop—with satisfaction*) Look, Anna—not a piece of work in the shop! And all that new lumber they bought—just stacked up— (*Makes clicking sound of commiseration.*)

ANNA

Someone might come in—

HEPZIBAH
(*With a shrug*)
We're just being neighborly.
(DANIEL *comes out of house—stops short.*)

DANIEL

Oh, I didn't know you were here—

ANNA
(*Embarrassed*)
Isn't anyone home?

DANIEL

Mother and Aunt Reba have gone to the country but Grandmother's home. Shall I call her?

96

FAMILY PORTRAIT

HEPZIBAH

Yes. We'd like to see her.
(DANIEL *exits.*)

HEPZIBAH

(*To* ANNA, *in a lower voice*)
Anyone seen Mary since Sunday?

ANNA

(*Shakes head "no"*)
I think she took it pretty hard. She'd bought a new shawl.
I talked to her the day he was coming home—and my, was
she excited!

HEPZIBAH

I know. I loaned her my dishes.

ANNA

Your *best* dishes?

HEPZIBAH

Not my best—but better than Mary has. The fuss that went
on here in this house—you'd think no other mother in Nazareth ever had a son!
(MARY *comes out, carrying* HEPZIBAH's *dishes. She is pale
and making an effort to be composed, and braces herself for the taunts she knows are coming.* DANIEL
*comes out behind her and goes over near the wall
and starts playing with a boat.*)

MARY

(*To* HEPZIBAH)
I'm sorry I'm so late returning your dishes—I meant to do
it before—

97

HEPZIBAH

It's natural you should forget—with all your other troubles
—I mean—so much to do, straightening things after—

MARY

Yes—I've—I've been quite busy—getting the house tidied
up—I sent the girls away with little Esther for a rest— (*A
pause*) And then Judah came home last night—

HEPZIBAH
(*Surprised*)

I thought he was staying away another month.

MARY

He left his job and hurried home hoping to see his— (*She
breaks off.*)

ANNA
(*Covering her slip*)

—to see Miriam? I suppose they'll be getting married before long—

MARY

Yes. It's all settled—I'm working on his things now. (*Indi-
cates sewing on table.*)

ANNA
(*With relief in her voice*)

Oh, well—with a good match like that, people are bound
to look up to you again— (*Breaks off, embarrassed*) I'm sorry,
Mary. I didn't mean to say that. (*Adds clumsily*) Jesus might
do better another time. We all have our off days. Ezra, the
singer, tells me that sometimes he can't get a full note. He—

98

HEPZIBAH

(*Interrupting*)

But he doesn't blame it on other people's lack of hearing!
I don't like to hurt your feelings, Mary—but I'm not one to
hold back anything. And I must say you always spoiled him.
Made him think he was something special—

ANNA

(*Defensively to* HEPZIBAH)

It's not easy to bring up a lot of boys without a man in the
family. (*To* MARY—*not unkindly*) You know, Mary, Jesus
really ought to have known better than to come back here
where everyone knows him. When a man's hammered on
your cupboard doors and mended your roofs, you're not going
to believe he's turned into a prophet overnight.

(DANIEL, *meanwhile, is climbing up onto the wall and
pauses, hearing this.*)

DANIEL

(*With sudden recollection*)

Are the police really after my Uncle Jesus?

MARY

(*Shocked*)

Why, Daniel!

DANIEL

(*Climbing onto wall*)

That's what they said in school. Why is everyone angry at
him? He whittled me a swell boat while he was here.

99

MARY

I don't know, Daniel. Your uncle does what he thinks is right.

(JOSEPH *starts down the staircase from the upper room, then stops abruptly as he sees the two women and pauses, unnoticed by them.*)

DANIEL

Well, I spit the seeds of a pomegranate out the window because I thought *that* was right and the other boys called me a sissy for not spitting them on the floor.

MARY

But being right doesn't always make everyone agree with you.

(DANIEL *now starts walking around the wall, balancing himself with outstretched arms like a tightrope walker. He sways unsteadily.*)

HEPZIBAH

(*With renewed malice*)

Well, Daniel—trying to do tricks like your Uncle Jesus?

MARY

(*With a gasp*)

Oh!

HEPZIBAH

(*Crosses to* DANIEL)

If you like magic, there's a wonderful fakir in town this morning—an Egyptian. You ought to see *him!* Makes flowers grow in a barren pot—tears a scarf in two and makes it all one piece again—

DANIEL
(*Balancing as he speaks*)
Oh, Grandmother—couldn't we see him?

MARY
(*Terribly moved*)
No, Daniel—

JOSEPH
(*Coming down*)
Get down, Daniel! How often do we have to tell you to keep off that wall! (*To* MARY) The boy'll break his neck one day. (*Pretends to see women*) Oh—hello, Hepzibah—Anna— I didn't see you. (*Yawns and stretches*) I'm late getting down this morning—we worked till after midnight getting a rush order through.

HEPZIBAH
Busy, eh?

JOSEPH
That isn't the word! It's been a grind. (*To* MARY) Did those new pegs come yet, Mother?

MARY
(*Blankly*)
New pegs?

HEPZIBAH
Well, I don't know where I got the idea but I thought things were kind of slack—

JOSEPH

(*Crossing to shop*)

Slack? That's good! (*To* MARY) The way we kept you awake pounding half the night!

MARY

(*Playing up—painfully*)

I'd—I'd better call Simon, hadn't I? If you're going to get busy at—at that job—

> (JOSEPH, *meanwhile, picks up hammer and starts pounding.*)

JOSEPH

(*From shop*)

Yes—tell him we haven't much time—

MARY

(*To women*)

If you'll excuse me—

> (MARY *is eager to get away but* DANIEL *defeats her purpose.*)

DANIEL

I'll go, Grandmother. (*Starts into house, calling*) Father! *Father!* Uncle Joseph wants you!

> (JOSEPH *hammers and whistles with a great pretense of busyness.* HEPZIBAH *smiles a little scornfully while* MARY *clasps her hands tightly together in acute misery.*)

ANNA

(*Embarrassed*)

We'd better be going—

MARY

Yes—I'm afraid we're all a little late getting our work done this morning. (*The two women start to exit, leaving the dishes*) Oh, Hepzibah—you forgot your dishes—

HEPZIBAH

Oh, yes—

MARY

And thank you.
> (*They exit. There is a pause, broken only by* JOSEPH's *hammering.*)

MARY

You can stop now, Joseph.

JOSEPH
> (*Coming out*)

You see, Mother—that's what we have to put up with all over town! (*Swings hammer.*)

SIMON
> (*Rushing out from house*)

Well, here I am, Joseph— (*Sees hammer*) Oh, got a job, have we? That's good! Who's it for?

JOSEPH

There isn't any job.

SIMON

Well, then why—

JOSEPH

Just a little show for the neighbors. Anna and Hepzibah were here.

SIMON

(*Crestfallen*)

Oh—I see. I thought for a moment— (*Breaks off.*)

JOSEPH

(*Swinging hammer*)

Feels nice—having a hammer in your hand.

SIMON

I'd do a job for nothing—I'm so sick of sitting around.

JOSEPH

Well, you can thank your precious brother for this.

SIMON

If only he *hadn't come back!*

MARY

(*Trying to control herself, she sits down under fig
tree and starts sewing* JUDAH's *shirt.* SIMON *sits next
to her.*)

You were all pretty excited when we heard he *was* coming
home. You were as pleased as anyone, Joseph.

JOSEPH

Of course I was! I thought he'd go over here the way he
did other places. If he *had*— (*Sighs*) Well, I guess it's easy to
fool strangers. (*He sits on a chair.*)

SIMON

He might have thought of what this would do to *us* before
coming back. Having your brother run out of town—

JOSEPH

(*With a shiver*)

I'll never forget the way they rose up against him in the synagogue and drove him out to the edge of that cliff! They'd have pushed him over, too, if—he hadn't got away.

SIMON

(*Lowering voice*)

Joseph, how do you suppose he did it? There was a lot of talk about his—well—just vanishing—

JOSEPH

His disciples slipped him away. (*Indignant anew*) And there's another thing! That crowd he got together for disciples. He couldn't pick people that might do him some good! A lot of ignorant fishermen! He'll never get anywhere with *them!*

MARY

Please, Joseph—do we have to have *that* all over again!

(MARY CLEOPHAS *comes out of the house,* DANIEL *following.* MARY *looks up with relief at the interruption.*)

MARY CLEOPHAS

Judah up yet?

MARY

He's having a good sleep. (*Looks up toward roof*) Poor boy—he needs it after that long trip. (*Pause*) My, but I'm glad to have him home again.

MARY CLEOPHAS

I should think you would be. At least he looks cheerful—

which is more than I can say for some of the faces around here. (JAMES *enters from stairs*) Oh, hello, James—
(JAMES *pauses at foot of stairs.*)

JOSEPH

I suppose we've got a lot to be cheerful about!

MARY

(*With tremendous effort*)

I—I think you're making all this even worse than it need be. These things blow over—

JOSEPH

That's easy to say.

MARY

Well, they do. People will talk about this—because it's the last thing that happened. And they'll keep on talking until something else comes along. It's always like that in a small town.

SIMON

It seems pretty unfair—

JAMES

(*Slowly*)

Just a minute, Simon. If Jesus had been a great success here—it would have helped you, wouldn't it?

SIMON

Of course.

JAMES

Well, that would have been unfair, too. I mean—you wouldn't have really earned it—but you would have taken it. I think you should accept it when it turns out this way, too.

106

JOSEPH

(*To* SIMON, *rising*)

Come on, Simon! I'm going to the store. (*To* MARY) Don't wait lunch for us.

DANIEL

Can I come too?

(JOSEPH *exits,* SIMON *following.*)

SIMON

I suppose so.

(DANIEL *runs out.*)

MARY

(*Following* SIMON *to gate*)

Simon?

SIMON

Yes, Mother.

MARY

Try to get Joseph into a good humor. I want things pleasant for Judah—his first day home.

SIMON

I'll try.

MARY

That's a good boy.

(SIMON *exits.*)

MARY

(*To* JAMES)

Thank you, James. It—it was nice of you to speak up—

JAMES
(*Clumsily*)
Right is *right*. (*Exits into house.*)
(*There is a moment's dead silence.*)

MARY CLEOPHAS
I sometimes wonder how Jesus would feel if, all the time he's preaching about peace and brotherly love, he knew the wrangling that's gone on in this house ever since he left.

MARY
(*Sitting—agitated*)
Oh, Mary Cleophas, I don't know—it's so difficult! (*Pause*) I've always encouraged Jesus and stood up for him but lately I've wondered if I was doing right—if I was doing my duty to my other children. After all, they've got *their* lives to live—they're entitled to their share of happiness. Goodness knows what they ask is harmless enough! Just work to support their families.

MARY CLEOPHAS
Yes—the way things are—I suppose you can't blame them for taking it pretty hard.

MARY
(*Reluctantly*)
People weren't in the right frame of mind for him to come back just now. No one here had any real faith in him. But their local pride was stirred up. Then when he came—and you know how simple he is—and he went around without making himself important—just living here as he always did —well, they just couldn't accept him—that's all.

MARY CLEOPHAS

I suppose they expected to have him wearing a gold crown.

MARY

(*Absently*)

Something like that.

MARY CLEOPHAS

Still, you've always treated him as though he were different from the others.

MARY

He *is* different. Even before he was born I knew he was different. I— (*She breaks off—rises and walks away, lost in a memory too deep to put into words. When she speaks it is about something else*) You know, I'm glad Judah didn't get home in time, after all. He loves his brother so—it would have hurt him to see how he was treated here. (*Pause*) Well, *his* life is going to be happy—Miriam is a lovely girl— (*She has a sudden thought*) Oh, I knew there was something I wanted to ask you. With the wedding coming on—I was wondering if you could lend me a little money.

MARY CLEOPHAS

Of course! How much do you need?

DANIEL

(*Jumping wall*)

Grandmother—the Rabbi and Mendel are coming to see you—I passed them on the road—

109

MARY

The Rabbi! And Judah not up yet! (*Smoothes her hair and dress, turns to* MARY CLEOPHAS) Am I all right?

MARY CLEOPHAS
(*Rises and nods*)

I'll open the gate.

MARY

I half expected Mendel, but not the Rabbi. I thought he was still away.
(MARY CLEOPHAS *opens the gate and* MENDEL *and the* RABBI *come in. Both look ill at ease.*)

MARY

Oh, Rabbi Samuel—I'm so glad to see you! And you, too, Mendel.

RABBI

Thank you, Mary.
(*There is an awkward pause.*)

MARY

My Judah came home late last night—I'm making him take a good sleep. But I'll call him now— (*Half turns to stairs.*)

MENDEL

No, Mary. The Rabbi wants to talk to you alone.

MARY CLEOPHAS

I'll go inside. How's business, Mendel?

MENDEL

Not bad.

FAMILY PORTRAIT

MARY CLEOPHAS

A marriage broker certainly has the edge on all the other trades.

MENDEL

How's that?

MARY CLEOPHAS

He's got Nature for a partner! Come along, Daniel.
(MARY CLEOPHAS *and* DANIEL *exit.*)

MARY

Can't I offer you some refreshments?

MENDEL

Well—

RABBI

I don't think so.

MARY

(*Sitting in a chair*)
A little glass of wine?

RABBI

What we've come to say isn't very pleasant, Mary. The quicker we get to it the better. (*He pauses, then turns to* MENDEL, *who remains standing next to him as the* RABBI *sits under the fig tree*) Shall I go on?

MENDEL

(*Relieved*)
Glad to have you.

RABBI

Aaron has called off the marriage between Judah and Miriam.

MARY

Called it off!

RABBI

Yes.

MARY

But *why?*

MENDEL

I hate to say this, Mary—and the words are my client's—not mine.

MARY

Go on.

MENDEL
(*Reluctantly*)

Your family is getting a bad reputation.
(*A long pause.*)

RABBI
(*Gently*)

Because of Jesus.

MARY

Oh, but that's so unfair! Why should the boy suffer for his brother!

MENDEL

That's just what we said to Aaron.

MARY

What did he say?

MENDEL

That things like this run in families. You can't tell where they'll break out next.

112

MARY

(*Rising indignantly*)

And we're supposed to stand by and do nothing? Well, I won't! I'll go to Aaron myself— (*Turns to gate;* RABBI *stops her.*)

RABBI

It's no use, Mary. He's closed his shop and taken his family away.

MARY

Didn't even give us a chance to defend ourselves.

(*The* RABBI *and* MENDEL *exchange a look.* MENDEL *signals the* RABBI *to speak.*)

RABBI

He did make one condition, Mary. Grudgingly—but he made it.

MARY

(*Hopefully*)

You mean—he might change his mind?

RABBI

If you meet this condition.

MARY

What is it?

RABBI

It's something *you* must do.

MARY

(*Eagerly*)

But I'll do anything! You know I will. Only tell me what it is!

RABBI

You must never receive Jesus here in this house again.

MARY

(*Incredulous*)

No!

MENDEL

That's what Aaron says—

RABBI

Disown him. Cast him off. Forget that he ever existed.

MARY

Oh— (*Sinks down on bench.*)

RABBI

It's a hard choice, Mary. But it's your responsibility. You're the one who must decide.

MENDEL

As far as I'm concerned the whole transaction is a total loss. My commission gone—my time wasted—to say nothing of the money I spent arguing terms. No place but in the wine-shop would Aaron discuss it! You know, this business of Jesus upset Aaron from the very beginning. He always said— "If he's a miracle worker—*I'm* a Roman Emperor!" I tried to tell him—Judah's a fine young man. Nothing like his brother. A little hot-tempered, perhaps, like all Nazarenes—but marriage will settle him down. I got him partly satisfied—then Jesus came back here with all that to-do about him and was a failure. That just finished Aaron!

FAMILY PORTRAIT

RABBI

Well, Mary?

MARY

My house will be open to Jesus as long as I live.

RABBI

It seems pretty hard for Judah to pay for his brother's mistakes. You said so yourself, Mary—

MARY

I can't understand it! Why did they all turn against him? What is he teaching that could possibly do anyone any harm?

RABBI

He excites the people. Puts a lot of new ideas in their heads. Starts them thinking. You see, Mary—it's so easy to get off on the wrong foot. Mind you, *I've* no objection to his teaching even though he isn't a rabbi. I don't even mind his allowing people to *call* him Rabbi. After all, it only means "teacher." I think he's honest and sincere. But very *indiscreet.* And when people criticize him, see what he says—"Don't judge people if you don't want to be judged yourself"—

MENDEL

But then he goes on to make it worse with a deliberate dig at the Pharisees—and you know how touchy they are—calling them names—insulting them! Tells them they're full of hypocrisy and corruption!

RABBI

Word about him has got to Jerusalem and right now, when things are so unsettled, it's a bad time to talk about the equality of man and the oppression of the poor. But that's the history of all reformers. They go too far. I don't want to worry you, Mary, but you mustn't close your eyes and your ears to the danger he's in.

MARY

(*Flaring up as she rises and walks across stage*)

That's all I've heard since the day he left home to preach! Everyone predicting he'd come to a bad end. And every day more and more people believe in him! Oh, what I've learned about human nature from this town! All my old friends and neighbors hardly able to wait until they get inside the gate to tell me some scandalous story about him! No wonder he was a failure here—surrounded by envy and hypocrisy and unbelief! And you—who invited him here— (*She breaks off, then returns and faces the* RABBI) You were always a fair man, Samuel—but now you've put yourself on the side of the Pharisees who hate Jesus because they see their power and their influence slipping away from them—because word of him and his work is spreading all over the country! That it's even reached Jerusalem! And it'll go on! People like *you* can't stop him! No one can stop him!

RABBI

(*Furious*)

I came here as a friend—trying to spare your feelings—I didn't come here to be insulted! (*Springs up and crosses to* MARY) Now, I'll tell you something! If someone doesn't get hold of that son of yours and stop him—he'll end up like his cousin John with his head on a harlot's platter. He's got the Temple and the Government so stirred up against him—

why, I wouldn't give you that—(*snaps his fingers*)—for his safety! Not that! (*Snaps his fingers again.*)

> (*There is a dead silence as the* RABBI *breaks off, breathless.* MARY *walks over to the gate and opens it and stands there.*)

MARY

(*Almost in a whisper*)

I don't like to ask a rabbi to leave my house—but I can't have you talking like that about my son. The streets are free—you can say what you like in them. But this is his home.

> (*Her voice breaks a little.* MENDEL *and the* RABBI *walk silently past her toward the gate.* MENDEL *exits but the* RABBI *pauses. He is profoundly moved and we must feel that he realizes her outburst was maternal, and not directed at him personally.*)

RABBI

I'm sorry, Mary. I lost my temper. (*Pause*) All I know is—if he were my son—I'd be worried.

> (*He exits after* MENDEL, *leaving* MARY *shaken by these last words.* MARY *is left alone on the stage and paces back and forth, her hands tightly clasped. Suddenly* JUDAH *comes from the roof-top and clatters happily down the stairs, talking as he comes.* MARY *turns, like one stricken. In her defense of* JESUS *she has forgotten all about* JUDAH.)

JUDAH

Mother! Why did you let me sleep so late? Half the day's gone and I haven't seen Miriam! (*He is at the foot of the stairs by the time he finishes and runs toward the gate.*)

MARY

(*Sharply*)

Don't go now! (JUDAH *halts*) I mean—I want a little visit with you myself. (*With an heroic effort at self-control*) Come and sit down by me—there's a good boy— (*She sits down under the fig tree.*)

JUDAH

(*Hesitating*)

I *did* want to see her—

MARY

After a while.

JUDAH

(*Crosses to her*)

You know how late it was when I got home last night? (MARY *nods*) I went the long way round so that I'd pass her house. It was all dark—but I knew where her window was— and I just stood there and looked and imagined her lying asleep with all her hair loose on the pillow— (*A pause as he sits down beside her*) Mother?

MARY

Yes, dear—

JUDAH

Now that it's so close I'm—I'm a little nervous about getting married. I mean—Miriam's so young—been so sheltered —and I don't know very much.

MARY

(*Choked*)

Oh, my dear!

118

JUDAH

I want to be a good husband—and I don't know how. I mean—I don't know all the things that make a happy marriage. I can't go to Simon or Joseph. They'd laugh at me.

(*There is a pause while* MARY *struggles to speak*.)

MARY

Do you love her so very much, Judah?

JUDAH

Why, *Mother!*

MARY

I mean—you're young—there are lots of other girls—

JUDAH

Other girls! I've been going to marry Miriam ever since I can remember!

MARY

Aaron is such a difficult man—always causing trouble—

JUDAH

Well, I'm not going to marry *Aaron!* And that reminds me, Mother. I wanted to tell you—Miriam and I decided a long time ago that we'd like to come here and make our home with you—that is, if you'll have us—

(MARY *puts her arms around him blindly for a moment, then rises abruptly*)

MARY

Judah, the Rabbi and Mendel were just here. They brought bad news.

JUDAH

What's happened? Is Miriam sick? What *is* it, Mother!

MARY

Aaron has called off the marriage!

JUDAH

(*Rising*)

But he can't do that! It's all settled—

MARY

(*Haltingly*)

Aaron's pretty influential. It isn't easy to go against him—once he's roused. Mendel and the Rabbi did their best—

JUDAH

(*Only half listening*)

But what have I done!

MARY

You haven't done *anything!* (*Searching desperately for reasons*) It's just that—Aaron's ambitious and—and we aren't exactly what you'd call a prominent family— (*She breaks off*) There's nothing we can do, Judah. He's taken Miriam away.

JUDAH

But there must be a *reason*, Mother—what is it? He must have said something. Mendel and the Rabbi wouldn't come here on just nothing! They wouldn't dare!

    (MARY *realizes that she can't evade the truth any longer. She faces* JUDAH *with as much courage as she can muster.*)

MARY

I don't know how to tell you! (*Puts her hand on his arm*)
The only one of my children who never gave me a moment's
worry! (*Pause*) Judah—he won't let you marry her—because
of your brother—

JUDAH

My *brother*?

MARY

Because of—Jesus.
(*There is a silence while* JUDAH *stares at her.*)

JUDAH

You mean they've called off my *wedding* because of Jesus?

MARY

Yes. (*She puts her arms around him*) Oh, Judah—I don't
know what to say to you—I know how hard this is on you!
It's hard on *me*, too—
(JUDAH *shakes her off, half mad with grief and re-
sentment. He is young enough to be nearly in tears.*)

JUDAH

It's easy to talk! But I'm young! And my life's going to be
ruined just because I've got a brother with crazy ideas!

MARY

Judah! Oh, I know how hurt and upset you are, dear—
but try to remember how fond you were of each other! Why,
Jesus was your favorite brother! He used to carry you
around—

JUDAH

I don't care what he was! He's ruined my life! (*Pause*)
Wasn't there *anything* you could do—

MARY

Aaron did make one condition—

JUDAH

Why didn't you tell me? What was it?

MARY

It was something impossible—

JUDAH

What *was* it?

MARY

He wanted us to disown Jesus—forbid him the house—

JUDAH

Well, why didn't you do it!

MARY

Judah!

JUDAH

What does he care about us! He goes his own sweet way—
running around the country doing as he pleases! Why should
we worry about him?

MARY

Judah—*don't!*

122

FAMILY PORTRAIT

JUDAH

I hate him! I *hate* him! I wish he were dead!

(*He brushes past* MARY, *flings open the gate and goes out into the road. The gate closes sharply behind him.* MARY *stands alone on the stage; then with a gesture of complete and utter defeat, she crosses with leaden feet to the table, sinks down on the bench and lays her head on her arms and weeps brokenly as—*

Curtain

ACT THREE

ACT THREE

Scene One

A street in Jerusalem. Night.

A very narrow square in a poor district. All across the stage are the fronts of houses. At downstage right is an arch leading to a small street. Upstage center is another small arch leading to another small street. At downstage left is a rising sideway leading to a third arch, also to another small street. A street lantern hangs from one of the houses at center. In the center of stage stands a small pump which is used as the neighborhood water supply.

The entire scene is lit by moonlight. MARY CLEOPHAS *is discovered sitting on the edge of the sidewalk near the pump. She has taken her shoes off and is rubbing one of her feet, talking as she does so to the two townswomen who are filling their pitchers.*

MARY CLEOPHAS

I'm a stranger here. My sister and I came to see my nephew. They're supposed to be having supper somewhere around here. My sister's trying to find the place. (*First* WOMAN *exits and she continues to the second*) I don't know as I'd care to live in a big city.

WOMAN

It's not very neighborly. And no place for the children to play but in the street. I'm always after my husband to move out into the country—at least, as far as Bethany.

MARY CLEOPHAS

We were there today. Some friends of my nephew's—it's a pretty little place.

WOMAN

Yes, it is. But this is nearer his work—and you know how men are. (*Her pitcher is filled—she lifts it up.*)

MARY CLEOPHAS

I don't suppose you know my nephew, do you? This is a big place—but he's quite a figure—from what they tell me—

WOMAN
(*Pausing*)

What's his name?

MARY CLEOPHAS

Jesus. Jesus of Nazareth.
(*The* WOMAN's *attitude changes. She puts the pitcher down with a clatter.*)

WOMAN

That man!

MARY CLEOPHAS

Then you do know him?

WOMAN

Don't insult me! I wouldn't have anything to do with him!

MARY CLEOPHAS

But I thought he created such a stir here last week—rode through the city—

128

WOMAN

Broke the Sabbath to do it!

MARY CLEOPHAS

But the people waved palms and cheered. I heard they made a real demonstration.

WOMAN

A lot of idlers and roustabouts! I haven't any use for him! Stirring people up—turning families against each other! Telling them what to do and what to say! Who does he think he is?

MARY CLEOPHAS

Did you ever see him?

WOMAN

I don't have to! I've heard enough about him.

MARY CLEOPHAS

I've known him since he was a little boy. I don't agree with everything he says. But he's a good and honest man.
(*The Roman soldiers' trumpet is heard offstage.*)

WOMAN

You wouldn't say that if you knew what he did here last week! Drove the money-changers out of the Temple with a whip! Where they've been since anyone can remember! That was a fine thing to do with old Annas getting a percentage on all the money that changes hands! And if that wasn't enough—he told them they could tear down the Temple—*tear it down, mind you*—and he'd rebuild it in three days!

MARY CLEOPHAS
(*Startled*)

He didn't say that?

WOMAN
(*With satisfaction*)

That and worse! He called himself the Son of God! A blasphemer! (*Long pause*) I maybe shouldn't have said so much—with you his relative—

MARY CLEOPHAS

Speech is free. I'm not one to stop anyone from speaking their minds. But I'm glad his mother didn't hear you. He's the apple of her eye. Besides, I've heard these things before and nothing ever came of it.

(*The Roman soldiers' trumpet is repeated offstage.*)

WOMAN
(*Roused again*)

He's going too far now! Even though they're used to fanatics here.

MARY CLEOPHAS

Fanatic—so that's what they call him!

WOMAN

And the class of people he has for followers! That red-headed dancer from Magdala—at least, that was *one* of her professions—

MARY CLEOPHAS

I've heard of *her.*

WOMAN
(*Acidly*)

She makes a show of herself! Breaking alabaster jars of perfume over his feet and bathing them with it and wiping them off with her hair!

MARY CLEOPHAS
(*Reluctantly*)

It does sound kind of pagan.

WOMAN

They tell me that back in Magdala she had more servants than she could count. Gold plates to eat off—and silk sheets to sleep under—

MARY CLEOPHAS

You don't say! (*Breaks off as she sees* MARY *approaching*) Here's my sister now— (*She rises*) Well—it's—it's been nice —having this little talk—good night.

WOMAN
(*Picking up pitcher*)

Good night. (*She eyes* MARY *curiously as she exits.*)

MARY CLEOPHAS
(*To* MARY)

Did you find it?

MARY
(*Wearily*)

No. And I looked at all the two-storied houses.

MARY CLEOPHAS

Two-storied?

MARY

Don't you remember—Selima said they were having supper in an upper room.

MARY CLEOPHAS

Oh, yes—

MARY

But there wasn't a sign of them. Then I had to turn back. There were soldiers pouring into the square.

MARY CLEOPHAS

Soldiers?

MARY

Roman soldiers. A lot of them. (*The trumpet is repeated offstage*) That's their signal again. They were being gathered from all over the city. It—it made me uneasy.

MARY CLEOPHAS

There's always something going on in Jerusalem. Especially at this season. You shouldn't have come here, Mary. You should be home where you belong with your family.

MARY

You've been wonderful. Stood by me when all the others went against me.

MARY CLEOPHAS

Well, I'm not so sure it was good sense.

MARY

You don't suppose those soldiers have anything to do with—with—

132

FAMILY PORTRAIT

MARY CLEOPHAS

Now, Mary, I know how important Jesus is to *you*—but they're scarcely calling out the Roman Army for him! (*Changing subject*) Sit down and rest. Those cobblestones!

MARY

(*Sits and looks around*)

If we only knew which house it was! And it's getting so late.

MARY CLEOPHAS

That woman Selima certainly got us on the wrong track! If we hadn't gone to her—

MARY

But it was *her* sons who made the arrangements for the supper—

MARY CLEOPHAS

The way she trails them around the country! Her James and her John! I should think it would drive them crazy. And what was that business about who'd sit where?

MARY

I didn't quite understand. Something about wanting to know when Jesus became king—if he'd promise seats on each side of the throne to her sons. (*Suddenly serious*) All this talk of thrones and kingdoms—he never cared for things like that— (*Breaks off*) I can't get those soldiers out of my mind!

MARY CLEOPHAS

If there was anything really wrong—wouldn't the girls have told us at Bethany? Surely, they'd be the ones to know —with him sleeping there every night!

133

MARY

Nice girls, weren't they? And they all seem so fond of Jesus. I'm glad he gets to a quiet place at night—and it's just walking distance from Jerusalem.

MARY CLEOPHAS

That Martha's a fine housekeeper. The other one moons around. Martha was telling me that it nearly drives her crazy. Meals to get for all those men—but do you think her sister helps? No—she just sits and admires Jesus and never lifts a finger. Martha even went so far as to complain to him about it—and what do you think he said? That Martha worried about the house too much—that her sister had her mind on better things! That's a fine way to talk about a lazy girl with her head in the clouds!

MARY

(*Not listening*)

You know, it's been years since I was in Jerusalem. But I don't remember it's ever being so—so unfriendly.

MARY CLEOPHAS

That's because you're tired.

MARY

(*Slowly*)

No. It's something else. Everything is so still—and yet it isn't peaceful. As if something were waiting. The way it is before a thunder storm. (*Adds impulsively*) You know, I thought once I got to Jerusalem I'd feel better, knowing he

134

was so close. But I don't. I shouldn't even say this, but for the first time in my life—I'm *frightened*.

(*Footsteps are heard offstage, then* JUDAS, *wrapped in his cloak, enters and rushes across stage.* MARY *rises quickly, speaking to* MARY CLEOPHAS *as she does so.*)

MARY

It's Judas! Judas Iscariot! He can tell us where they are! (JUDAS *halts at the sound of his name.* MARY *goes to him*) My, but I'm glad to see you! We've been searching for hours!

JUDAS
(*Almost wildly*)

Searching?

MARY

For Jesus and the others! They're having supper near here, aren't they?

JUDAS
(*Confused*)

Yes—they are. But it's so late—

MARY CLEOPHAS

That's what *I* said. We could have stayed comfortably at Bethany and seen him tomorrow. But she thought something might happen—

MARY

You know how *you'd* feel. Is he all right?

JUDAS

Why, yes—of course—

MARY

If he is in any danger you've got to tell me. I've come all this distance—

JUDAS

Everything has been going on as usual.

MARY

But they say he is upsetting law and order in Jerusalem—

JUDAS
(*Evasively*)

People use words lightly.

MARY

And that he breaks the Sabbath!

JUDAS

He doesn't know the meaning of time.

MARY

You're hiding something from me! What is it?

MARY CLEOPHAS
(*Chidingly*)

Mary! After all, his safety must mean as much to Judas as it does to you— (*To* JUDAS) She's been so worried.

MARY
(*Barely hearing* MARY CLEOPHAS)

He isn't in trouble—with important people, that is—who might do him some harm?

136

JUDAS

(Haltingly)

It's—it's hard to say—such a mixed crowd here in Jerusalem. You're bound to offend someone—sooner or later. Of course, he knows he runs that risk—but he won't listen to anyone— *(His voice trails off.)*

MARY

When did you see him last? Did you have supper with him and the others?

JUDAS

I left early.

MARY

Oh, then they're still there! *(To* MARY CLEOPHAS*)* We'll get to him after all!

MARY CLEOPHAS

Is it very far?

JUDAS

About fifteen minutes' walk.

MARY CLEOPHAS

Fifteen minutes! *(To* JUDAS*)* All right, lead the way.

JUDAS

I can't. I'm—I'm—in a hurry. I have an errand— *(His voice trails off.)*

MARY

If you'll just tell us how to get there—

JUDAS

(Quickly and nervously)

You go down that way—*(points across stage)*—until you

come to a wide cross-street—and there's a fountain in the middle—a square one. You turn left there and go straight along until you reach the street of the water-sellers—

MARY CLEOPHAS

How'll we know it?

JUDAS

There're always donkeys tied to the racks.

MARY CLEOPHAS

Not at *this* time of night!

JUDAS

(*Desperately*)

There'll be a lot of water jars standing about. You can't miss it!

MARY CLEOPHAS

Now let's get this straight. I've had all the wrong directions I want in one evening. (*She repeats directions slowly, to his intense nervousness*) We go down that way—(*points*) —until we get to a wide street. (*She stops*) I didn't know there *were* any wide streets in Jerusalem.

JUDAS

I mean—wider than this.

MARY CLEOPHAS

—and there's a fountain—

JUDAS

(*With increasing emotion*)

Then you turn left—

138

MARY CLEOPHAS

—and find the street of the water-sellers. And the house is there. Which house is it?

JUDAS

The third house—it has a balcony. (*He turns to go.*)

MARY CLEOPHAS

What's the man's name?

JUDAS

Nathan!

MARY

(*To* MARY CLEOPHAS)

Can't you see he's in a hurry? (*To* JUDAS) Don't worry about us. We'll find it quite easily now. (*Pause*) I hope we haven't made you late.

JUDAS

(*In a strangled voice*)

No. There is still time.

MARY CLEOPHAS

Good night.

MARY

Good night. And thank you. (*Takes his arm*) And you're sure no harm can come to him?

JUDAS

He says no one can destroy him.

MARY CLEOPHAS

What does he mean by that?

139

JUDAS
(*With growing panic*)
I don't know! *I don't know!* (*He rushes from scene.*)

MARY CLEOPHAS
Another fifteen minutes!

MARY
Oh, it doesn't matter—now that we know where we're going. (*They start to cross stage*) I'm so glad that Judas left early!
 (*As they exit, the soldiers' trumpet sounds offstage and is answered from a distance.*)

Curtain

ACT THREE

Scene Two

A house in Jerusalem. Night.

This is the upper room in the house of NATHAN, *the water-seller (a replica of da Vinci's painting of the Last Supper). It is small in size. In the upstage back wall are three windows with practical shutters looking out on the roof across the street. At downstage right is a curtained opening apparently coming from the lower floor of the building. There is also another entrance farther upstage right. Corresponding openings, stage left. In the center is a long table, set for thirteen people, and there are hassocks, stools, etc. On the table are candlesticks with the candles still burning, a large silver goblet and a flagon of wine. The tablecloth is white with a blue design. At downstage left is a big closet or dresser for plates, etc. Above this closet is a small window.*

The stage is empty at rise of curtain. Then MARY *and* MARY CLEOPHAS *enter through the door at downstage right and stare around the empty room.*

MARY

(In great disappointment)

Oh, we're too late! They've gone!

*(*MARY CLEOPHAS *goes to the table and looks at the food.)*

MARY CLEOPHAS

Not long, though. The best thing we can do is sit down

and wait. Someone'll be coming along to clear the table. (MARY *starts, indecisively, to cross toward a seat.*)

MARY

If we'd only been a few minutes sooner! Or if we knew where they've gone.

MARY CLEOPHAS

You see, Mary—I was right. We shouldn't have come.

MARY

Oh, I'm so disappointed! I *counted* on seeing him!

MARY CLEOPHAS

Better sit down and rest awhile.

MARY

I—I don't know as we ought to stay. After all, we're strangers. They might not like to walk in and find us sitting here.

MARY CLEOPHAS

I don't like to be disagreeable, Mary, and I'm not one to complain— (*Pauses, then adds with a dry smile*) Well—not overmuch—but I'm not going to walk one more step on those cobblestones until I know where I'm going—and *why!* (*Sits down.*)

MARY

There must be somebody around here who can tell us—I wish we'd asked Judas what his errand was. That might have given us some idea. (*Walks restlessly to table*) I hope they gave him a good supper!

MARY CLEOPHAS

I hear someone coming.

MARY

Maybe he's come back! Don't say anything about what a hard time the boys are having. Anyway—not at first.
(*She turns expectantly. The door opens and* MARY MAG-
DALEN *enters, pausing in surprise and alarm. She is
plainly dressed but carries her clothes with a certain
air. She has beautiful red hair.*)

MAGDALEN

What are you doing here? Who let you in?

MARY

Why, no one. The door was unlocked.

MAGDALEN

Who are you looking for at this hour of the night?

MARY CLEOPHAS
(*Irritated*)

Are you the woman of the house?

MAGDALEN

No, I'm not. Who do you want to see?

MARY

We're looking for Jesus of Nazareth.

143

MAGDALEN

Who told you he'd be here?

MARY

Judas. He showed us the way—

MAGDALEN

Judas! I thought he'd gone with the others—

MARY

We met him in the street alone.

MAGDALEN

Where was he going?
>   (MARY CLEOPHAS *regards* MAGDALEN *curiously and edges closer.*)

MARY

He didn't say. He seemed in a great hurry. He just told us how to get here— Surely this is the place. (*Pause*) Hasn't Jesus been here?

MAGDALEN
> (*Again secretive*)

They've all gone.

MARY CLEOPHAS

Why, I know who you are! You're from Magdala, aren't you?

MAGDALEN

I *was* from Magdala.

144

FAMILY PORTRAIT

MARY CLEOPHAS

Selima told me about you.

MAGDALEN

Selima talks too much. Who are you?

MARY CLEOPHAS
(*Gesturing toward* MARY)

This is the mother of Jesus.
(MARY *is startled to find who this woman is—while*
MAGDALEN *is dismayed at learning* MARY's *identity*.)

MAGDALEN

Oh—I'm—I'm so sorry—I had no idea—
(*The two women face each other for a moment—then*
MARY *advances, her hand out.*)

MARY

I'm glad to know you. I've heard about you— (*Breaks off*)
You're a friend of my son—
(MAGDALEN *is genuinely touched by* MARY's *gesture, but*
before she can reply—)

NATHAN
(*Voice offstage*)

Magdalen! Magdalen!

MAGDALEN
(*Turning*)

Yes—
(*She goes to door—opens it, admitting* NATHAN.)

145

NATHAN

(*Mystified*)

They bought swords tonight! Jesus told them to even sell their clothes if they had to—but to get swords!

MAGDALEN

(*Giving warning look*)

You're just in time to meet some friends of Jesus! Well, not friends, exactly. This is his mother and— (*She looks questioningly to* MARY CLEOPHAS.)

MARY

And my sister.

NATHAN

I never thought about his having a family!

MARY

Is anything wrong? Anything about my son?

MAGDALEN

No. Just something about the house. Nathan is the proprietor here. It was he who made all the arrangements for the supper tonight—

NATHAN

And he'll never get a better one! Not if he lives to be a hundred! Fit for a king!

(*The Roman soldiers' trumpet is heard, offstage.*)

MARY

The Roman soldiers!

146

MARY CLEOPHAS

My sister met some in the street.

NATHAN

(*Alarmed*)

What were they doing?

MARY

Getting orders to go somewhere.

NATHAN

Did you hear where?

MARY

Why—yes, I did. Let me think. (*Pause*) Is there someone here called—Pilate?

MAGDALEN

Yes—there is.

MARY

Well, it was his house they were going to.

MAGDALEN

(*Again warning* NATHAN)

Probably to quiet some disturbance. There's always something happening in Jerusalem—especially at this time of the year—holiday crowds—

NATHAN

I don't believe you ladies had better wait here. There's no telling when he'll be back—

MARY CLEOPHAS

I'm not going another step for anybody!

FAMILY PORTRAIT

MARY

But where has he gone?

NATHAN

They've just gone for a walk. In the hills, I guess.

MAGDALEN

They often go up Gethsemane way. There're some gardens there.

NATHAN

I'm full up—haven't any rooms. I could give you the address of another place—

MAGDALEN

(*Sharply*)

You can't possibly turn them out at this hour of the night! Let them wait here. I'll be responsible. (*To* MARY) They're very strict about closing time for eating houses—

NATHAN

Yes—that's it.

MAGDALEN

But don't worry. You can stay right here.

MARY CLEOPHAS

That's good sense!

MARY

If he's gone to the gardens—maybe I could look for him there. (*To* NATHAN) I don't like to inconvenience you—

MAGDALEN

It's a hard, rough road—besides, you'd never find it in the

148

dark. I know what we *could* do—(*to* NATHAN)—we could send your boy with a message—

NATHAN

It's getting pretty late—

MAGDALEN

Oh, he won't mind. Tell him to— (*She breaks off and turns to* MARY) Wouldn't you like to talk to him yourself—tell the boy just what to say?

MARY

Yes. I would.

MAGDALEN

(*Moving to door with her*)

He's down in the kitchen. Show her the way, Nathan.
(*As she exits,* MAGDALEN *turns back to* MARY CLEOPHAS, *her manner one of urgency and warning.*)

MAGDALEN

You must get her out of Jerusalem!

MARY CLEOPHAS

(*Startled*)

What's that?

MAGDALEN

Get her away from here! Take her home!

MARY CLEOPHAS

You mean—there's going to be trouble?

149

MAGDALEN

Yes.

MARY CLEOPHAS

What kind of trouble?

MAGDALEN

None of us knows! That is, none of us—except—

MARY CLEOPHAS

Except who?

MAGDALEN

I think Jesus knows. He tried to tell the disciples tonight. To prepare them. (*Pause*) He was like a man going on a far journey.

MARY CLEOPHAS

Then she must see him before he goes—

MAGDALEN

It's not safe for her to stay here. Not safe for anyone who is close to him—

MARY CLEOPHAS

I begged her not to come! But I couldn't stop her. No one could. I never saw her like that before. It's as if she knew something was going to happen. I tried to tell her he was all right—but since we got here, I haven't been so sure. (*Suddenly remembers*) Tonight while I was waiting for Mary in the street, I asked a woman if she knew him. Well, I knew he wasn't popular with everyone—but the things she said about him! I was glad his mother didn't hear them! And this woman who had never seen him—acted as though she *hated* him!

MAGDALEN

His most bitter enemies are people like that. People who've never heard him speak—who don't even know what he teaches. But they're afraid he'll upset the old order of things. So, because they fear him—they hate him.

MARY CLEOPHAS

But if he knows all these things—why does he stay?

MAGDALEN

He says he must wait until what is written has been done.
(MARY *enters, relieved at having sent the message.*)

MARY

Well, the little boy has gone to tell him that we're here. I *do* feel better—

MARY CLEOPHAS

That's good! Now perhaps you'll sit down and rest yourself. (*To* MAGDALEN) She's been on her feet the whole day— and we're neither of us getting any younger.
(MARY *sits on a stool in front of the table.*)

MAGDALEN
(*To* MARY)
Is this your first visit to Jerusalem?

MARY

Oh, dear, no. I came quite often as a girl. And then when my children grew up, I came with them. I've even been to Egypt!

151

MAGDALEN

Really? I've never traveled *that* far.

MARY

I didn't care much for it. But my husband—he was a carpenter—he got a lot of building ideas. (*Pause*) If you're not
too busy, I wish you'd stay and tell me about my son. I'm
so *hungry* for firsthand news of him.

MAGDALEN

I'd love to. (*She starts to move a hassock from around
table so she can sit.*)

MARY CLEOPHAS

We hear such mixed-up stories back home. He says one
thing here in Jerusalem and by the time it's repeated all the
way to Nazareth—well, you can imagine how it sounds! So
she had to come and find out for herself.

MARY

I've always tried to think of my other children. To see
their side of it. Suddenly I couldn't any longer. It was as
if they all just—melted away. I didn't have any other children. Only this one—and he was in trouble.

MAGDALEN

(*Discovering cloak on hassock*)

Oh, he's left his cloak!

MARY

(*Holding her arms out for it*)

Isn't that just like him? Never thinks of himself. But I
don't see why all those disciples can't think of him once in
a while.

MARY CLEOPHAS

Oh, they're too busy worrying about themselves! Who'll sit at the right hand and who'll sit at the left! So he goes out in the cold without a cloak! Just let something go wrong—when you get into trouble you find out who your friends are!

MAGDALEN

He knows that. That's what makes him so wonderful.

MARY
(*Taking cloak*)

And it's torn, too! If I had a little thread I could mend it while I was waiting—

MAGDALEN

Leah usually keeps some up here. (*She looks around*) Oh, I know—it's in the next room. (*She exits right.*)

MARY CLEOPHAS
(*Rising and crossing to her*)

Mary, I think we ought to go home—back to Nazareth, I mean—

MARY

Without seeing him!

MARY CLEOPHAS

Well—no—but as soon as you do—

MARY

Oh, once I've seen him I'll do whatever he says.

153

MARY CLEOPHAS

This is no place for us to be.

MARY

But you were the one who didn't want to go any farther—

MARY CLEOPHAS

Well, I feel differently now.

MARY

(*Gestures toward room at right*)

Not because of *her?*

MARY CLEOPHAS

No. She's a real nice woman. You'd never think she'd led that kind of life.

MARY

S-sh—she'll hear you!

MARY CLEOPHAS

There must be something to the things he teaches—to change a person that way.

MAGDALEN

(*Returning*)

Will this do?

MARY

(*Taking it*)

Oh, yes—it's good and strong.

(MARY *sits down with cloak.* MARY CLEOPHAS *sits again.*)

154

FAMILY PORTRAIT

MAGDALEN
(*Moving candelabra*)
There, I think you'll have enough light.

MARY
(*Starts to sew—looks up with smile*)
How this takes me back! When he was a little boy his
knees went through everything! He played so hard. And
when he grew up and went into the carpenter shop he
worked the same way. Never knew when it was time to stop.

MAGDALEN
(*Sitting down near* MARY)
He's the same now. Works until he drops. He has so much
he wants to say—he seems almost afraid he won't have time
to say it. (*She quickly covers this ominous note by adding*)
The other day it grew dark without his even knowing—and
the people stayed on and listened—way into the night.

MARY CLEOPHAS
(*Yawning*)
He always was a good talker. It's a real gift.

MARY
What did he talk about that time?
(MARY CLEOPHAS *nods*.)

MAGDALEN
About a shepherd who lost one sheep. And how he left
the whole flock and searched and searched the night through
until he found it. And how happy he was and what it meant

155

to him to bring one—to bring one lost sheep back into the fold. I love that story.

(MARY CLEOPHAS *falls asleep.*)

MARY

How I wish I could have been here and heard these things! But I feel easier in my mind about him—talking to you. Please tell me more. Do great crowds gather when he preaches?

MAGDALEN

I should think so! You know how fond he is of children? Well—the other day when he was preaching, a lot of them gathered around and someone complained. But Jesus said if having the children running about shouting and laughing while he preached annoyed the older people—then *they* could leave. That Heaven itself was made up of the innocent and the simple-hearted.

MARY

(*Hesitantly, looking around at her sleeping sister-in-law*)

There's something I want to ask you—while my sister's asleep. I want to ask you—about the miracles.

MAGDALEN

I—I can't say much about the miracles. They just *were*. (*Pause*) Of course, he performed a great many more in the beginning when he first started out on his work. But lately he's turned more and more to teaching. Telling people the way to live. And a great deal about understanding and forgiveness. And the beauty of human life. I don't believe he thinks miracles are very important. He always says a man isn't really any better after seeing something spectacular than

156

he was before. He'd much rather talk about loving them that hate you than raise the dead. After all—he's not concerned with the death of the body. But the disciples—they'd like more miracles. Excitement—and the crowds. But he does less all the time. There is one thing he wants them to believe above everything. It underlies every word he says—it is the very foundation on which his whole teaching is built.

MARY

And what is that?

MAGDALEN

The dignity—and the greatness of man. People criticize him for calling himself the Son of God. They forget how much more often he calls himself the Son of Man. Because Man is God—and God is Man.

(*The Roman trumpet is heard outside.* MAGDALEN *rises in instinctive alarm.* MARY *sees this and puts her sewing down.*)

MARY

You feel you owe a great deal to my son, don't you?

MAGDALEN

Without him I am nothing.

MARY

Then you must tell me the truth about him. Is he in danger?

MAGDALEN

(*Searching for an evasion*)

There is no greatness without danger.

157

MARY

But why? But why? What does he *say* or *do* or *teach* that anyone could possibly find fault with?

MAGDALEN
(*She sits—then speaks almost bitterly*)

He blesses the poor and the meek. And the hungry. And those who weep. And he tells them all the same thing—rich and poor alike. "If you love me—take up your cross and follow me."

MARY
(*Apprehensively*)

Cross?

MAGDALEN

That's a figure of speech he uses. He means—self-denial. (*Pause*) And then—he blesses those who have sinned. I—I don't want to—to embarrass you—or bore you by telling you about myself. You probably know already—

MARY

Only what I've heard—and you can't judge people by that.

MAGDALEN

You looked just like him as you said that. But, you see, it's his acceptance of people like me that they condemn! This whole idea of repentance and forgiveness. No one ever taught it before. Being *born* again! Think what that means!

MARY

I can *see* what it means.

MAGDALEN

He raised me from the dead. I was blind—and now I see.
I was deaf—and now I hear. The world will never be the
same because he has lived!

> (MAGDALEN, *overcome with emotion, sinks down, her
> head in her hands.* MARY, *seeing her shivering, puts
> the cloak of* JESUS *around her shoulders, then takes
> the silver chalice from the table and offers it to*
> MAGDALEN.)

MARY

Drink a little of this wine. It will warm you.

> (MARY *holds the chalice to* MAGDALEN's *lips. In the
> silence that follows we hear the Roman soldiers'
> trumpet repeated—then suddenly the growing mur-
> mur of a crowd.* MARY *and* MAGDALEN *look at each
> other. Neither speaks. Now there is shouting and an
> angry rise to the voices outside. Both women are
> rigid with fear.* MARY *puts the chalice down on the
> table with a trembling hand.*)

MARY CLEOPHAS
(*Awaking*)

What's that? Someone call me? (*Neither* MARY *nor* MAG-
DALEN *answers.*) They're certainly worked up over something—

> (*The noise grows in volume and nearness. Suddenly
> the name* "JESUS OF NAZARETH" *is clearly heard
> shouted derisively.* MARY *springs to her feet and
> rushes to the window. At the same moment,* NATHAN
> *bursts into the room.* MAGDALEN *rises, the cloak of*

JESUS *falling to the stool.* MARY *is at the window when* NATHAN *seizes her and thrusts her away.*)

NATHAN

Get away from that window! They've arrested him! I don't want my house mixed up in this!

MARY

Arrested!

NATHAN

They're taking him to Pilate.

MAGDALEN
(*To* NATHAN)

How did they know where he was? Who told them?

NATHAN

Judas Iscariot.

MAGDALEN

Judas! But the other disciples—what were they doing?

NATHAN

Running for safety!

MARY CLEOPHAS

Deserted him—

MARY
(*Stunned*)

Arrested! I must go to him!

FAMILY PORTRAIT

MARY CLEOPHAS

(*Trying to make her voice gentle*)

No, no! They've only trumped up some charge against
him—

(NATHAN *exits as* MAGDALEN, MARY *and* MARY CLEOPHAS
cross to the door. MARY *makes no answer to her sister.
At the doorway she stops, turns and goes across the
room to the hassock, and picks up his cloak.*)

MARY

He'll need this. They may keep him all night.

(*As she starts again for the door the shouts in the
street reach a crescendo and* MARY *stands,* JESUS' *cloak
clasped in her arms as she hears the words—"Crucify
him! Crucify him!"*

Curtain

ACT THREE

Scene Three

The house at Nazareth.

It is late afternoon, nearly dusk on a warm day in mid-Summer. The fig tree is heavy with green leaves and purple fruit. From the carpenter shop come occasional sounds of someone working. NAOMI *is busy at the table under the fig tree. There is a small oil wick burning in a little basin and there are two seven-branched candlesticks on the table, unlighted, with a taper beside them. The table is spread with a fine cloth and* NAOMI *is putting some plates and bowls on it. She moves rather quickly, humming a little to herself. The temper of the scene is happy. They are all more prosperous—relaxed. As her back is turned to the wall,* DANIEL, *now a lad of sixteen or so, vaults the wall and lands in the courtyard with a clatter.* NAOMI *turns with a start.*

NAOMI

Be *careful,* Daniel! You'll fall one day and hurt yourself!

DANIEL

(*Laughing*)

Mother, you've been saying that to me ever since I can remember and I've never hurt myself yet! I just saw Uncle Judah hurrying down the street. Is he looking for old Beulah?

FAMILY PORTRAIT

NAOMI
(*Nodding*)

They expect the baby any time now. (*Looks at him*) Daniel, go right in and change your shirt. It's a sight!

DANIEL

But I only put it on clean this morning!

NAOMI

This is afternoon and we're having company for supper. *Important* company. Now, hurry!

DANIEL

Esther's young man? I heard Uncle Joseph talking about him.

NAOMI

Since you *know*—all right. Now get yourself clean and *stay* clean.

DANIEL

Oh, all right!
　　　(DANIEL *exits into the house.* NAOMI *crosses to the car-
　　　penter shop and calls.*)

NAOMI

Simon!
　　　(SIMON *appears with some work in his hand.*)

SIMON

What is it, Naomi?

NAOMI

Don't you think it's time you got washed and dressed?

163

SIMON

Is it late?

NAOMI

No—but everyone in the house will want to get ready at the same time. There won't be enough hot water to go round, and we don't want any fuss—especially with Judah's baby being born. I must say I think Deborah might have waited a day.

SIMON

I'll just finish this and then I'll come.
  (*Before* SIMON *can return to the shop,* REBA *comes out at top of stairs and rings a bell.*)

NAOMI
(*To* SIMON)

You see! She's calling Joseph!
  (SIMON *lays his work down on a bench at the entrance to the shop and goes into the house with* NAOMI. *They talk as they go.*)

SIMON

Have you got my clean things ready for me?
  (REBA *comes downstairs.*)

NAOMI

Everything's laid out.

SIMON

Wait a minute.

REBA
(*Calling*)

Esther! Esther! Are you ready yet?

FAMILY PORTRAIT

ESTHER'S VOICE
(From upstairs)
I'm fixing my headdress. Wait till you see how it looks!

SIMON

Isn't that a new dress?

NAOMI

Do you like it? I only have to put on my shawl when I hear them coming.

> (SIMON *and* NAOMI *go into the house. There is a short wait and then* ESTHER, *now grown into a charming young woman, comes running out. She is wearing her hair braided like a coronet; over it a pale blue veil.*)

ESTHER

Look, Mother! Isn't it lovely? Grandmother wore it when she was a girl. Oh, I'm so happy. (JOSEPH *enters through the gate as she speaks*) Father! How do you think I look?

JOSEPH
(With loving pride)
My, but you look pretty! Like your mother the day we became engaged. Do you remember it, Reba?

REBA
(With a laugh)
Of course I do. I'm not so old that I've forgotten it! Go on, Joseph, get those dirty clothes off. Our guests should be here soon. Did you know—they're coming all the way from Damascus by camel?

JOSEPH

(*Crosses and kisses* ESTHER. *He is softer—mellower*)
By camel? Are they *that* rich? I always wanted to travel by camel. (*Lowers his voice*) By the way, have you warned Esther not to mention—you know?

REBA

Yes—she understands. (MARY *appears at top of stairs*) Be careful—here comes your mother.

JOSEPH

Ah, there you are, Mother! Had a nice rest?

MARY

I haven't been resting. I've been with Deborah. Poor child, she's so uncomfortable this hot day.

REBA

Do you think it will be soon?

MARY

Who can tell? A baby comes when it gets ready. Is Beulah on the way?

JOSEPH

Judah's gone for her. (*To* REBA) I'll hurry and change. (*He exits into house.*)

MARY

(*Smiling*)
I can't get used to it! *My* baby rushing after a midwife for *his* baby! (*Pauses*) It's nice, though. I never get over

being grateful that Judah found a good wife after all. (*Another pause*) Nearly time for the guests, isn't it? (*With a smile for* ESTHER) Someone's getting impatient.

ESTHER
(*Shyly*)
They say he's very handsome.

MARY
(*In mock surprise*)
Handsome? Why, it seems to me someone said he was cross-eyed and had a hare lip—and walked with a limp. (*Turns to* REBA) Isn't that right, Reba?

REBA
(*Playing up to her*)
That's what *I* heard.

MARY
Still—it wouldn't matter, would it—if he had a good character? (*Pinches* ESTHER's *cheek affectionately; then turns suddenly to* REBA) Oh, Reba, will you take a look in the kitchen and see how the supper is getting on? (REBA *exits.* MARY *turns to* ESTHER) Happy? (ESTHER *nods;* MARY *adjusts the headdress just a shade*) There—that's better. (*Puts an arm about* ESTHER) Why—you're trembling! (*Sits down with her*) Here now, we can't have that. There's nothing to be afraid of.

ESTHER
(*With a little gulp*)
I'm going to live so far away.

167

FAMILY PORTRAIT

MARY

Damascus *is* a good ways off—but, just think! You'll be head of your own house—no old mother-in-law to make life miserable, the way I do around here. (*She smiles at* ESTHER *who smiles back a bit shakily*) And then, before you know it, your babies will be coming along. Wait till you have your first one! Nothing makes you feel so important as your first baby. I'll never forget mine. . . . (*She breaks off—a shadow crossing her face*) Look—there's the first star! Like the one at Bethlehem— (*Pause. Throws off mood with effort*) There now, don't let me start talking about—about when I was young—or the company won't get any supper! (*Hearing footsteps outside the gate*) And here they are now! (*As* ESTHER *hurriedly exits calling "Mother, Mother!"* MARY *calls to house*) Joseph! Reba! Here they are!

(NAOMI *and* SIMON *come from the house, followed by* REBA *and, lastly,* JOSEPH. *There is a knocking at the gate.* JOSEPH *waves the others back.*)

JOSEPH

I'll go.
(*Before he can get started, the gate swings open and* JUDAH *enters with* BEULAH, *the midwife, at his heels.* JOSEPH *speaks in a disappointed tone.*)

JOSEPH

Oh, it's *you!*

JUDAH
(*Laughing*)
That's a fine greeting for a prospective father.

168

JOSEPH

I didn't mean it like that. I thought it was our guests from Damascus and I rushed out only half-dressed.

JUDAH
(*To* MARY)

I thought I'd never find Beulah. Half the women in Nazareth picked out today to have babies. (*To* BEULAH) Hurry upstairs, will you, Beulah? You know the way.

BEULAH

With my eyes shut!

MARY

Do you need any help?

BEULAH

Not yet. If we do later, I'll call you. (*Starts up the stairs.*)

JUDAH
(*Calling after her*)

Be sure you make it a boy!

BEULAH
(*Turning on stairs*)

I'll do my best—but you should have thought of that sooner. (*All laugh.* BEULAH *continues upstairs.*)

JOSEPH
(*To* REBA, *smoothing his clothes*)

Am I all right now?

REBA

You look fine.

(JOSEPH *gives his cloak a last twist and walks across the courtyard with something of a swagger just as* MARY CLEOPHAS *appears at the gate. She has a jug of wine.*)

MARY CLEOPHAS

Who's this prancing around like a peacock? (JOSEPH *swings around*) Oh, it's Joseph. (*She turns to* MARY) I brought the wine. How are you going to have it—hot, with spices?

MARY

I think so. Yes—since we're going to eat outside we'd better have it *hot*.

MARY CLEOPHAS

I can't think why *anyone* wants to eat outside! You never know what's going to fall in your food. (*To* JOSEPH, *as he walks about*) For Heaven's sake, Joseph, light somewhere! You're not the bride!

(*Before* JOSEPH *can think of an answer the gate is flung open and* MENDEL, *the marriage-broker, rushes in and stands panting in the middle of the courtyard.*)

MENDEL

(*Between gasps*)

They're here! I ran all the way from the market place— soon as I got out of their sight! I'm all out of breath! Someone give me a drink!

MARY CLEOPHAS

I knew he was leading up to that.

(REBA *pours wine from the jug and hands the cup to*

MENDEL. *He drinks it in short gulps, while they all wait impatiently.*)

JOSEPH

Somebody go in and tell Esther.

NAOMI

I'll go.

JOSEPH
(*To* MENDEL)

Where are they now?

MENDEL
(*Between gulps*)

At the Inn. Leban wouldn't hear of anyone seeing to his camels but himself. Special grain and all that. Spends money like a prince. And the boy! Handsomer than ever!

JOSEPH

Shouldn't we have gone to meet them? After all—they're strangers here.

MENDEL

Make us seem too anxious! I've left my assistant to show them the way. (*Sees* ESTHER *coming from the house*) Ah— there she is! Looking like a picture! (*Beams on* ESTHER) I saw a big sack full of presents for I wonder whom! You're a lucky girl!

REBA

All the luck isn't on our side, Mendel. You don't see a girl like Esther every day.

MENDEL

There's luck on both sides. That's what makes it a good deal.

> (MENDEL *suddenly thinks of something. He turns to* JOSEPH *and speaks inaudibly.* JOSEPH *nods.* MENDEL *looks relieved. During this action* MARY CLEOPHAS *adjusts* ESTHER'S *veil.* MARY *watches* JOSEPH *and* MENDEL *closely. As* MENDEL *turns away,* MARY *speaks with quiet emphasis.*)

MARY

Mendel!

MENDEL

(*Apprehensively*)

Mary! Oh, I'm sorry—I didn't see you in all the rush. My, but you're looking well—and on a busy day like this! Your hands full with the engagement supper—and if I remember your housekeeping rightly, it'll be something to make our visitors open their eyes. (*Rattles on nervously*) I'll never forget—

MARY

(*Interrupting in a quiet voice*)

Never mind about the supper, Mendel. (*A hush falls on the group*) When you first met Leban and his son in Damascus last year—did you tell them all about our family?

MENDEL

(*Eagerly*)

I should say I did! What a wonderful woman you are— what a fine man their father was, God rest him! (*Switches subject cannily*) I was thinking this morning—if he could

172

only have lived to see this day! Esther was just a baby when
he died, wasn't she?

MARY

(*Quietly*)

She wasn't born.

MENDEL

(*Abashed*)

Oh, I thought she was.

MARY

You're sure you told them about everyone?

MENDEL

I was at my best! You should have heard me! I went back
five generations. I got them so tangled up in the family tree—

MARY

You left no one out?

(*Before* MENDEL *can reply there are three sharp raps at
the gate.* MENDEL *is tremendously relieved.*)

MENDEL

They're here!

(*There is a general scurry.* ESTHER *goes close to her
mother.* JOSEPH *goes to the gate.* MARY *detains* MEN-
DEL.)

MARY

You haven't answered me, Mendel.

MENDEL

(*In a desperate whisper*)

Why stir that up again, Mary? You're a respectable family.

You've lived it down. (*As* JOSEPH *opens the gate* MENDEL *rushes forward; speaks at gate*) Leban!
> (MARY CLEOPHAS *has come close to* MARY, *an expression of pity on her face.*)

MARY CLEOPHAS

I'd be awfully sure I was right before I said anything, Mary.
> (MARY *nods.* MARY CLEOPHAS *pats her arm. The visitors,* LEBAN *and his son, are entering the courtyard. There are ad lib greetings between the men.* LEBAN's *son steals glances at* ESTHER, *who has moved over to one side, alongside her mother.* MENDEL *is asking whispered questions of his assistant, who carries the parchment of the betrothal agreement. Then* JOSEPH *steps forward, avoiding* MARY's *glance.*)

JOSEPH

I'd like you to meet our womenfolk. Mary, my mother—and Mary Cleophas, my aunt—my wife—my sister-in-law—and my daughter, Esther! (LEBAN *and his son bow in time with each introduction.* ESTHER *gives one pleased look, then drops her eyes.* JOSEPH, *anxious to get them all in the house, is overhearty as he adds*) And now—shall we go into the house and have a little glass of wine? Then we must go over the contract once more, just to make sure everything is all right. What do you say?
> (*There is a murmur of assent.*)

MENDEL

I have suggested a little change. That if any of the donkeys are in foal their young are included in the dowry.

JOSEPH

Yes, yes, of course!

MENDEL

And very good luck if they are—sign of a large family. I'll make that change when we get inside.

JOSEPH

Then, when everything's signed, our young people here— (*indicating* ESTHER *and* LEBAN'S *son*)—can have a little chat and get acquainted.

MENDEL

(*With professional sentiment*)

Well, if looks mean anything they're not exactly strangers— even *now!*

(*There is general laughter. The young couple look confused and embarrassed.* JOSEPH *gestures toward the house.*)

JOSEPH

It's cool inside—

MARY

Just a moment, Joseph. (*To* LEBAN) I'm sorry to interfere at the last minute like this—but since no one else will speak, I'm afraid I'll have to. I can't let this go on without saying something.

MENDEL

Please, Mary—don't be unreasonable!

MARY CLEOPHAS

Be quiet, Mendel.

(JOSEPH *looks at his wife and makes a helpless gesture.*)

175

LEBAN
(*Puzzled*)

I don't understand.

> (*There is a buzz of whispering among the family.*
> MARY *silences it with a little gesture. A dead silence*
> *follows.*)

MARY

What I have to say isn't easy. You see—(*there is a painful*
pause)—we had a little trouble in our family— (*She falters.*)

LEBAN

Yes?

> (MARY *summons her courage and forces herself to a*
> *complete statement in one sentence. As she speaks*
> *the light begins to slowly soften.*)

MARY

My oldest son—he got into some difficulty with the authorities.

LEBAN
(*Hesitantly, to* MENDEL)

Is that James—the one who's away?

MARY

No, not James. The one I mean is dead. (*Pause*) He was
killed.

LEBAN

Oh, I'm sorry. An accident?

MARY

They thought he was trying to stir up trouble and they—
they crucified him.

176

LEBAN

Crucified him!

MARY

(*With sudden desperation*)

Don't you understand? Don't you see what I'm trying to tell you? My son was Jesus of Nazareth! (*Her voice breaks and she makes a gesture of helplessness and turns away.*) Now you know!

> (*There is a long pause.* LEBAN *looks questioningly from one face to another but the family avoid his gaze, not knowing that he is trying to conceal the fact that the name means nothing to him. Suddenly,* JOSEPH *breaks into the silence, anxiously.*)

JOSEPH

(*Eagerly, in a rush*)

You're not going to let this come between the young people, are you? After all, it's a long time ago, and outside of that, no one can say a word against us. Everything we told you about our family is true.

MENDEL

Absolutely true!

JOSEPH

(*Continuing*)

I admit we did leave that out—about my brother. Maybe we shouldn't have—but my daughter's happiness means a lot to me. (*His voice breaks a little*) I didn't want to spoil her chances.

> (MARY CLEOPHAS, *who has been watching* LEBAN, *breaks in.*)

MARY CLEOPHAS

Save your breath! The man's never heard of him!
> (*The others stare at* LEBAN *with incredulity. He mumbles in his embarrassment.*)

LEBAN

Well—you see—I'm afraid—I—I—I live so far away—

MARY

He was quite well known.
> (*The family is upset, a little indignant, over* LEBAN's *ignorance of their tragedy.*)

MARY CLEOPHAS

Well known? He was the talk of the country! When he came to a town you couldn't find a place to sleep—

JOSEPH
> (*Breaking in*)

Do you remember that time in Capernaum? (*To* LEBAN) We heard so much, we went there to see him—and the place was *packed!* We couldn't even get *near* him! Imagine! His own family!

SIMON
> (*Proudly*)

He made towns important that no one had ever heard of before. And he'd have all kinds of offers from neighboring places.

JOSEPH
> (*Also with pride*)

And then, he was always a guest at the local synagogue.

178

He'd preach there on Sundays. He was a *big* attraction!

LEBAN

He was a rabbi?

MENDEL

Not a regular rabbi.

SIMON
(*Quickly*)

They called him that.

MARY

He wasn't interested in what people called him. That's one
of the things he tried to teach his disciples.

LEBAN

He had *disciples*?

MARY

They hung on every word he said—

SIMON

—when things were good. But they didn't stand by him so
well when he got into trouble—

MARY CLEOPHAS
(*Explosively*)

Stand by him! They ran like rabbits!

MARY

I hear that some of them are keeping on with the work.
I *hope* it's true. It'd be a shame to have it all lost. He worked
so hard—never took any care of himself. You know—looking
back—I've often thought he knew he wasn't going to live
long.

SIMON
(*Slowly*)
There was some talk of people seeing him again—*after*—

MARY
I used to wait for him. I thought surely if he came anywhere it would be here, to his home. But he never came.

LEBAN
(*Kindly, seeing her emotion*)
What did he teach?

MARY
Why—to—love your enemies—never to judge or condemn
anyone—to be *forgiving*. And to make life as easy as you
could for other people. (*Pauses, groping for the most important things*) To live for a purpose in which you believe and
never let anyone keep you from your belief—not even your
own family. You must be willing to die for it. And not to be
afraid of people who—who kill the body. Because, after that,
there is nothing more they can do. And to be kind to little
children—he loved little children. (*A pause in which she feels
she must make this last point dreadfully clear—and searches
for the right words*) And to remember always that human life
is beautiful—and noble—because it houses God. (*She is aware
of the little startled look on* LEBAN'*s face—and hastens to ex-
tend the idea*) I mean—when—when you degrade or dishonor human life—you degrade and dishonor God. (*There
is a moment of dead silence*) That was all he taught.

LEBAN
Has anyone ever tried it—to live the way he taught?
180

MARY

I don't think so.

LEBAN

Might be interesting to see what would happen if they did.

MARY CLEOPHAS

It's too simple!

MARY

You know, I think that's what caused all the trouble. They couldn't understand that it was all just as simple as that. That there wasn't something behind it. So they accused him of trying to attack the government.

LEBAN

(*Relieved*)

Then it was a political offense?

MARY

I guess you'd call it that. (*With embarrassment*) I—I never really quite understood. (*Pause*) They hurried me out of the city. I think he told them to. I never saw him again.

(*There is a rap at the gate.*)

MENDEL

It's the Rabbi! (*Hurries to gate*) Now we can get down to business.

(JOSEPH *and* LEBAN *prepare smiles for the* RABBI. *The tempo of the scene becomes brisk.*)

RABBI

(*Entering*)

Well, well. How's everything?

JOSEPH

Fine! (*He glances at* LEBAN *who makes no denial*) Just fine! (*To the others*) How about that glass of wine now?

> (*They all assent, with ad lib lines and introductions, and the men go into the house first, with* REBA *and* ESTHER *following, leaving* MARY, NAOMI *and* MARY CLEOPHAS *on the stage.*)

NAOMI

Where's Daniel? I just know that boy hasn't changed his shirt!

> (*She exits as* JUDAH *comes down the stairs.*)

JUDAH

Everything go all right, Mother? Did they sign?

MARY CLEOPHAS

They're just doing it.

JUDAH

That's fine.

MARY CLEOPHAS
(*To* JUDAH)

Well, how are things going?

JUDAH

A little slow.

MARY CLEOPHAS

Then it'll be a boy! They're unobliging—even before they're born! (*She exits, leaving* MARY *and* JUDAH *alone.*)
> (*There is a silence.*)

182

FAMILY PORTRAIT

MARY
(*With careful casualness*)
If the baby's a boy—what are you going to name him?

JUDAH
We haven't decided.

MARY
I wish—

JUDAH
What, Mother?

MARY
Will you do something for me, Judah?

JUDAH
Of course I will! What is it?

BEULAH'S VOICE
(*From upstairs*)
Judah!

JUDAH
(*Calling up*)
Coming!
   (*He starts toward the stairs,* MARY *going a step or two
   with him. He stops on the first step.*)

MARY
(*Looking up as she speaks*)
If it's a boy, will you name him after your brother— (*Hesi-
tantly*) After Jesus, I mean?

JUDAH

Why—why, yes, Mother. I'll talk to Deborah about it—
(*He leans over the railing of the staircase and kisses her.*)

MARY

It's a nice name. (*As* JUDAH *starts to run up the stairs, she adds*) I'd like him not to be forgotten.

> (MARY *is alone. The light has faded and it is nearly dusk. She turns and goes toward the table, picks up the taper and starts to light one of the seven-branched candlesticks. As she does this—*

Curtain